TWEETS from TAHRIR

TWEETS
from
TAHRIR

Egypt's revolution as
it unfolded, in the
words of the people
who made it

Edited by NADIA IDLE
and ALEX NUNNS

OR BOOKS
New York

First published by OR Books, New York, 2011
www.orbooks.com

Copyright in this collection Nadia Idle and Alex Nunns
Individual Tweets copyright the Tweeters

Foreword copyright Ahdaf Soueif: 2011

ISBN Paperback   978-1-935928-45-4
ISBN E-book   978-1-935928-46-1

Library Of Congress Cataloging-in-Publication Data
A CIP Record is available for this book from the Library of Congress

British Library Cataloguing-in-Publication Data
A CIP Record is available for this book from the British Library

Printed by BookMobile in the United States of America
Printed in the United Kingdom by CPI Books Ltd

Dedicated to the Egyptian revolutionaries

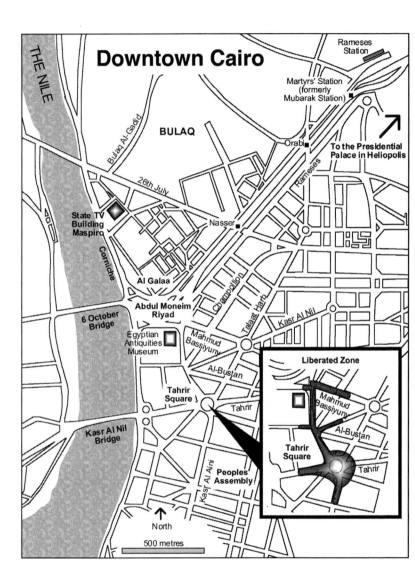

CONTENTS

Foreword		9
Preface		13
Introduction		17
1:	The Spark	25
2:	The Day of Revolt	31
3:	Keeping the Streets Unsettled	47
4:	Anticipation	53
5:	The Day of Rage	59
6:	The Vanishing State	65
7:	Not Intimidated	77
8:	"The Army and the People are One Hand"	87
9:	The Million Man March	95
10:	Bloody Wednesday	101
11:	Fortress Tahrir	121
12:	The Day of Departure	135
13:	The People are in Charge	149
14:	A New Threat	159
15:	The Wael Ghonim Interview	165
16:	Momentum Regained	177
17:	The Revolution Deepens	187
18:	Fury	193
19:	The Friday of the Martyrs	207
20:	The Cleanup	225
21:	Epilogue	231

FOREWORD

Ahdaf Soueif

I THINK WE'RE AGREED: Without the new media the Egyptian Revolution could not have happened in the way that it did. The causes were many, deep-rooted, and long-seated. The turning moment had come – but it was the instant and widespread nature of the new media that made it possible to recognize the moment and to push it into such an effective manifestation.

What happened next has already become legend. Lines and images from the three weeks that followed January 25, 2011, have imprinted themselves not just on the Egyptian psyche but on the memory and imagination of the world.

I have friends on antidepressants who, over the twenty days of revolution, forgot to take their pills and have now thrown them away. Such is the effect of the Egyptian Revolution.

On Friday, February 11, the day Mubarak fell, Egypt partied. Chants and songs and drums and joy-cries rang out from Alexandria to Aswan. The defunct regime was only mentioned in reference to "we want our money back."

Otherwise, three chants were dominant – and very telling: One – "Lift your head up high; you're Egyptian" – was a response to how humiliated, how hopeless we'd been made to feel over the last four decades.

The second was: "We'll get married. We'll have kids," and reflected the hopes of the millions whose desperate need for jobs and homes had been driving them to risk their lives to illegally cross the sea to Europe or the desert to Libya.

The third chant was: "Everyone who loves Egypt, come and rebuild Egypt."

And the next day, they were as good as their word: They came and cleaned up after their revolution. Volunteers who arrived on Tahrir Square after midday found it spick and span, and started cleaning up other streets instead. I saw kids perched on the great lions of Qasr el-Nil Bridge buffing them up.

I feel – and every parent will know what I mean – I feel that I need to keep my concentration trained on this baby, this newborn revolution – I need to hold it safe in my mind and my heart every second – until it grows and steadies a bit. Eighty million of us feel this way.

Eighty million at least – because the support we've been getting from the world has been phenomenal. There's been something different, something very special, about the quality of the attention the Egyptian revolution has attracted: it's been – personal.

People everywhere have taken what's been happening here personally. And they've let us know. And those direct, positive, and emotional messages we've been receiving have put the wind in our sails.

We have a lot to learn very quickly. But we're working. And the people, everywhere, are with us.

It remains to be seen whether the tools that helped achieve the impetus and immediate success of the Revolution will also help in the tasks that lie ahead: building consensus, building institutions, mending the damage, and molding the future.

PREFACE

AS AN EGYPTIAN WATCHING the live images of Tahrir Square on her computer at work in London, Nadia Idle, one of the editors of this book, could no longer take it. After much hesitation and several false starts, one irrepressible drive took over all other thoughts; she just had to be there. She booked a flight, told one friend, and sent an email to her boss a few hours before getting on a plane on the night of February 7, 2011.

All the things that had worn her down to the point of leaving Egypt – the unrelenting harassment of women, the lack of civic pride, a people whose broken soul seemed to permeate any human interaction, day in and out – seemed to have evaporated. Tahrir was a space of unity, pride, resistance, celebration, laughter, sharing, and most importantly ownership. This was the People's space; our rules and our demands. We would not leave until justice was born.

Meanwhile, back in England, Alex Nunns, the other editor of this book, was transfixed by events. The twenty-four-hour news channels had cameras stationed on top of buildings overlooking Tahrir, so the revolution really was televised. But he found that the most compelling coverage was on Twitter, coming directly from the people in the square. The tweets were instant, and so emotional and exciting that anyone following them felt an intense personal connection to what was happening in Tahrir.

This book is an immediate attempt to document a fraction of those remarkable messages before they disappear into the vacuum of cyber-space, and to allow the story of this historic uprising to be told by the people who made it happen.

The tweets are valuable for two reasons: as firsthand, real-time accounts of events (a primary source for historians of the Egyptian Revolution); and as testimony to the significant role that Twitter and other social media played in those events.

It is important to say up front that we do not claim that this collection is comprehensive. It is merely a sample of some of the activity that was taking place on Twitter. To print every tweet that related to the uprising would take several volumes. One activist alone managed to tweet 60,000 words during the revolution! Neither do we claim to have included all of the key tweeters who took part. We are bound to have overlooked some and underrepresented others.

Rather, we have sought to present a readable, fast-paced account of the Revolution that gives a sense of what was being said on Twitter. At the core of our approach are several key people whose tweets run right through the work. We hope the reader will get to know them (because remarkably their personalities do come across in messages of 140 characters) and follow their different journeys as the Revolution unfolds. Aside from this core group, many other tweeters make less frequent appearances. Our intention was to begin the account with just a few voices, and broaden it out as the days passed, reflecting the progression of the demonstrations themselves as more and more people joined.

We have concentrated on tweeters in Cairo. The Revolution happened across Egypt, with particularly strong movements in Suez and Alexandria. Whole books could – and should – be written about these struggles, but the epicenter of events was in the capital. We also chose not to include tweets from important players who were outside Egypt. For example Mona Eltahawy, an Egyptian writer living in New York, was very active promoting the cause on Twitter and relaying information back to those in Egypt, but she was not reporting from the ground.

For logistical and stylistic reasons we have used only English-language tweets, meaning some popular tweeters who write predominantly in Arabic, like Wael Abbas, have not been included. It may surprise readers in the West to see so many Egyptians tweeting in English. In Egypt, those with laptops and smart phones are the more affluent in society, among whom the use of English is quite common. These were the people who discussed the events online, although on the ground they were part of a much wider movement that included the urban poor.

Throughout the book we have been true to the original tweets. We have not corrected any grammar or spelling mistakes. They appear here as they appeared on Twitter. Arabic words have been transliterated in many different ways and we have not adjusted them for consistency.

The editing process involved selecting tweets to tell a story. Some may feel that in doing so we have imposed our own narrative onto events. In fact this is always the case when any story is told or any history book is written. We believe this new approach to documenting history is in some ways less guilty of the offense, because all of the reporting is directly from the people involved and written as it happened. Alternative narratives could be constructed by using different tweeters who opposed the Revolution or thought the protesters were going too far. This book is not about them, it is about the people who changed the world, although the criticism of others is sometimes referred to by the tweeting protesters.

In fact our approach to editing has closely resembled the experience of Twitter users themselves. From the mass of available sources on Twitter, the user must select the tweeters they want to follow, and then read the messages as they come through. Just as an editor discounts tweets that are irrelevant or unimportant, so the Twitter user skims over them to the next valuable tweet. Often several people will be giving their perspective on the same event or topic. There will be inconsistencies, but the narrative that forms in the reader's mind is an amalgamation of these different perspectives.

To reflect that process of constructing knowledge, we have been faithful in reproducing the time of the tweets to the second – even where this has harmed the flow of the book when somebody made an important point that was off-topic. Similarly we have not vetted the tweets for accuracy. Sometimes rumors were tweeted that turned out to be wrong, but this is an important part of the social media experience. It is fascinating to see falsehoods debunked as different players chime in with their own information.

Because the protesters in Tahrir were united around a set of demands, we found that political infighting was minimal. Where we did find disputes we included them for interest and not because of any agenda on our part. We did not attempt to represent the various groups in proportion to their strength, as a detailed analysis of the political forces at work in the Revolution would take a different kind of book.

The brief introductions to each chapter are intended to give the vital context that is not always available from the tweets. For insights into the internal dynamics of the protesters, particularly in the early stages, we are indebted to Gigi Ibrahim, an activist and key tweeter who had the patience to talk it through with us, although of course responsibility for the interpretation we have presented is all ours.

We would like to thank every tweeter whose words appear in this book. All of them were kind enough to give permission for their tweets to be printed. The amount of enthusiasm they have shown for this project has blown us away.

Finally, we make no apology for being supporters of the Egyptian Revolution. What we saw in Tahrir and read on Twitter inspired us. We hope that, through this book, it will inspire you too.

Nadia Idle and Alex Nunns, March 2011

INTRODUCTION

THE EGYPTIAN UPRISING has been described as a "Twitter Revolution." It was not. Revolutions do not come out of thin air, or even cyberspace. But the internet provided a tool that helped shape the form of the uprising, and it gave us some of the most riveting real-time coverage ever recorded.

Since the wave of revolts that swept the Arab World starting in December 2010, commentators have struggled to explain a phenomenon none of them saw coming. Searching for a distinctive factor at play, many have settled on Facebook and Twitter, aspects reassuringly familiar to their own lives. In an inevitable backlash, others have pointed out that revolutions happened long before computers were invented.

What has sometimes been missing from the debate is close analysis of what the revolutionaries actually used social networks for. In the case of Twitter it was primarily used as an alternative press. It was a means for those on the ground to report what was happening for the benefit of their fellow Egyptians and the outside world, and a place for emancipating bursts of self-expression.

Of course, the internet was also an organizing tool. Calls for protests and coordination between the different groups that mobilized for the January 25 demonstrations in Egypt, which started the Revolution, did happen online. Facebook was the network most suited to the task, where information could be spread to thousands of people in an instant and then shared between friends. This dissemination was far faster than leaflets, with the added benefit that those receiving the messages were already interested and trusted the source.

Planning discussions also took place on Twitter, using the hashtag #Jan25 to enable anyone to join the conversation, and activists talked to each other directly using the @ reply function. Later on, once the Revolution was in full swing, protesters used Twitter to announce new initiatives, like marching on the parliament building, and to boost their collective morale with reports of other developments around the country.

But Twitter came into its own as a place to report on events. Initially, Egyptians were avid recipients of such reports coming out of Tunisia. Later their own accounts of the Egyptian Revolution would help inspire uprisings across the region.

That Twitter was used in this way, for news, was no coincidence. Many tweeters considered themselves "citizen journalists" and made it their mission to get the word out with (usually) accurate bites of information and a flow of videos and pictures. Professional journalists also used the site (some of them like Ashraf Khalil are included in this book) as did more opinion-orientated bloggers. The result was like a company of artists painting a constantly updated picture of events.

The importance of citizen journalists cannot be overestimated in a country like Egypt with a state controlled media. One of the features of the uprising was the gradual undermining of state TV and newspapers, to the extent that journalists began to resign as the public saw the ludicrous coverage for what it was. Also instrumental in this process was the contrast provided by transnational satellite TV channels like Al Jazeera, whose reporting was often influenced by information and footage coming from citizen journalists on the ground.

The activists on Twitter were not only talking to their fellow Egyptians but to the international media and the world. They went to great lengths to get online during the five-day internet blackout, when their tweets could not easily be read by other Egyptians. By telephoning friends abroad to upload their tweets, pooling their resources to get on to the one remaining internet service provider in Egypt (the one used by the stock exchange), or offering interviews to news organizations in return for access to their satellite internet connections, activists managed to ensure that the regime could not cut them off from the world.

The fact that Hosni Mubarak's regime took the step of blocking the internet, despite the millions of dollars lost to the economy, is a testament to the fear it provoked among the rulers. This is where commentators who seek to downplay the role of social media come up short. Their argument that social upheavals happen periodically, and that a great many have been very successful without Twitter, is obvious. But every revolution is different, shaped in part by the technology available to those who make it and those who try to stop it.

Soon after printing presses became widespread in England, the English Civil Wars of 1642–51 happened. There was lots of discussion and hype about the role that popular pamphlets from agitators like "free-born" John Lilburne were playing. The government's response (both that of Charles I and later Oliver Cromwell) was censorship. The same thing has been repeated ever since. The tactic does not always work, but those in authority would not try it unless they thought it might.

In Egypt it did not work. By the time the regime blocked the internet on January 28 it had already lost control. While the internet was down the most decisive battle occurred between protesters and the state's security forces on January 28 and a Million Man March was held on February 1. The Revolution was already tangible, it was escalating spontaneously. There was no need to organize events online because people were spending every day face to face on the streets. The demands and tactics of the Revolution were being determined by the spontaneous chants of the people.

There is a certain arrogance to the lazy Western description of a Twitter Revolution. It excuses commentators from seeking to understand the deep-seated causes of the uprising – the brutal economic reality for the majority of the population, the imposition of neoliberal policies reducing job security and suppressing wages, the lack of opportunities for educated young people, the sheer vindictiveness of a Western-backed dictator as expressed through his police gangs.

It ignores the role of the urban poor, many of whom literally placed their bodies between tyranny and freedom on the front line. For the unemployed and those living on two dollars a day, Twitter and Facebook were the last things on their minds.

It ignores the role of the organized working class which had been striking since 2006 and whose refusal to go to work in the days before Mubarak resigned finally removed the last plank from under his regime.

And it ignores the years of thankless work by the very activists who made such good use of Twitter during the uprising and whose words fill this book. They had been mobilizing, forming groups, and holding small protests in the face of police brutality since at least the year 2000, but the world had hardly noticed. And they are still doing so now, as the Revolution continues to unfold.

There is a clip on YouTube of a young Californian woman being asked about events in Egypt in a vox-pop. In her account the protests happened because the Egyptian government blocked the internet. She got the entire causal relationship the wrong way around. But she was not so far away from those who say that Twitter and Facebook are the reason for the revolts.

The Arab uprisings would not have happened at the speed and in the manner in which they did without social media. That we can say. And the way in which the Revolution is seen in the West, in the Arab world, and even within Egypt would be very different if we had not been able to hear from protesters and see the action so directly.

But the Revolution would not have happened at all without the Egyptian people deciding enough was enough and putting their lives on the line for justice, dignity, and the hope of a decent future.

1

THE SPARK

...as the Tunisian Revolution inspires the Arab world

 Gsquare86 Gigi Ibrahim حبيبي
The Tunisian revolution is being twitterized...history is being
written by the people! #sidibouzid #Tunisia

ON FRIDAY JANUARY 14, 2011, *Tunisia's dictator of twenty-four years, Zine al-Abidine Ben Ali, was forced from power after weeks of unprecedented popular protest. An electric shock zipped through the region.*

It had begun when Mohamed Bouazizi, a twenty-six-year-old fruit seller from the town of Sidi Bouzid on the Mediterranean coast, set himself on fire on December 17, 2010. Bouazizi's story resonated with millions living under corrupt regimes – humiliated by the state, unable to make enough money to survive, he finally snapped when police officers spoiled his fruit, confiscated his weighing scales and beat him up. He went directly to the local governor's office and, when nobody would see him, doused himself in petrol and set himself alight. He died eighteen days later.

Protests flared up in Sidi Bouzid and soon spread to the Tunisian capital. Bouazizi's actions were the catalyst, but the depth of Tunisia's problems was shown as all sections of society, from labor unions to lawyers, joined the revolution.

Things were changing in the Arab world. Power structures that had been fossilized for over half a century were now confronted by a young population with few opportunities and endless frustrations.

In Egypt conditions were ripe for an uprising. The country had its own high-profile testimony to appalling state brutality – the killing of Khaled Said, a young man who, according to witnesses, was beaten to death in public by police in June 2010, his head slammed against the marble stairs and iron door of a building and his body dumped by the roadside. His family said he had been targeted because he had video evidence implicating police in a drug deal. In response, a Facebook page was set up called We Are All Khaled Said. It provided a rallying point for Egypt's youth.

The formal opposition parties to Egypt's thirty-year president, Hosni Mubarak, had failed. Now new activists were to the fore, emerging from solidarity with the second Palestinian intifada of 2000, protests against the Iraq War in 2003, and the wave of strikes that had gripped Egypt since 2006.

These events had given rise to a spectrum of social movements from the anti-Mubarak Kefaya ("enough") group formed in 2004, to the April 6th Youth Movement, inspired by a textile strike in the town of Mahalla that was violently put down by police in 2008, to the Revolutionary Socialists with links to the workers, to the reformist National Association for Change associated with Mohamed ElBaradei, launched in 2010. All these groups coordinated online.

With new technology the old regime had lost its control over information. The Tunisian Revolution was watched in Egypt and across the Arab world, not on state TV but on satellite channels like Al Jazeera and Al Arabiya. People no longer had to read stifled accounts in state-run newspapers when they could go on the internet and hear from Tunisian protesters directly through social networks.

Gsquare86 Gigi Ibrahim حبيبة
The Tunisian revolution is being twitterized...history is being
written by the people! #sidibouzid #Tunisia
17:28:11 Jan 14

 Gsquare86 Gigi Ibrahim حبيبة
BEN ALI LEFT just confirmed through Aljazeera
19:25:19 Jan 14

 tarekshalaby Tarek Shalaby
VIVA LA REVOLUCION!!! RT @SultanAlQassemi: MY GOD!
MY GOD! This is AMAZING.
19:27:12 Jan 14

 tarekshalaby Tarek Shalaby
WE WILL FOLLOW! RT @SultanAlQassemi: Tunisians are
the heroes of the Arab world.
19:29:27 Jan 14

 Gsquare86 Gigi Ibrahim حبيبة
goooose bumps alll over ..i can't believe i lived through an
arab revolution !! thank you #Tunisia
19:43:40 Jan 14

 amuchmoreexotic Ben
I don't understand how the people of Tunisia overthrew their
government without me signing an e-petition or changing my
Twitter avatar.
20:49:01 Jan 14

 mosaaberizing Mosa'ab Elshamy
Dear people watching Arabs Got Talent, there's a better show
going on called Tunisia's Got Freedom. Watch that.
21:02:46 Jan 14

 TravellerW Mo-ha-med
Tonight some ppl will go to bed thinking"I helped free my
country today". #Tunisia's activists & demonstrators,we salute
you.
00:59:10 Jan 15

ManarMohsen Manar Mohsen
A Facebook event for a revolution in Egypt: http://on.fb.me/
hQioSl. Don't forget to RSVP. ("Maybe" if you're still unsure of
your schedule).
19:21:27 Jan 15

Gsquare86 Gigi Ibrahim جيجي
The black and white days are coming, there is no grey
15:00:42 Jan 16

Gsquare86 Gigi Ibrahim جيجي
A MAN IN #EGYPT SET HIMSELF ON FIRE CHANTING
AGAINST STATE SECURITY IN FRONT OF PARLIAMENT
AT 9:00 AM TODAY #Sidibouzid #Revolution attempt?
10:40:52 Jan 17

3arabawy Hossam عمو حسام
people r setting themselves on fire. i suggest they burn down
police stations and torture factories instead.
10:58:21 Jan 17

Gsquare86 Gigi Ibrahim جيجي
is this true a 3rd person lights himself on fire at parliament for
the 2ND TIME TODAY!?! #Egypt #Sidibouzid
13:03:28 Jan 18

norashalaby Nora Shalaby
I think it is time for Mubarak to set himself of fire. He is the
one who really deserves to burn #egypt #fuckmubarak
13:57:35 Jan 18

Gsquare86 Gigi Ibrahim جيجي
There is nothing that #Mubarak can do now to prevent the
madness that will end his regime..IT WILL HAPPEN THIS
YEAR!! #DownWithMubarak 2011
16:05:36 Jan 18

monasosh monasosh
There is something incredibly sad abt ppl setting themselves
on fire in a fatal hopeful/desperate attempt to be heard!
19:15:45 Jan 18

Gsquare86 Gigi Ibrahim جيجي
#Jan25 I hope we can get over the logistics and just take to
the streets in masses all over #Egypt
22:28:35 Jan 20

monasosh monasosh
Did we finally settle on a tag for 25th of january?
16:41:11 Jan 21

Gsquare86 Gigi Ibrahim جيجي
I still haven't decided from which place I will be tweeting live
coverage on #jan25 , if u have a suggestion DM me
22:26:57 Jan 21

monasosh monasosh
What time should we be in the streets tomorrow #jan25?
09:57:06 Jan 24

Sandmonkey Mahmoud Salem
For when and where the revolution will be and other improtant
info, go here http://bit.ly/Jan25egypt
21:51:18 Jan 24

Ghonim Wael Ghonim
Despite all the warnings I got from my relative and friends, I'll
be there on #Jan25 protests. Anyone going to be in Gam'et
Dewal protest?
22:13:48 Jan 24

monasosh monasosh
Scared, excited and hopeful #Jan25
23:30:48 Jan 24

TravellerW Mo-ha-med
Yes, I'm worried about tomorrow. Which is exactly why I am
going - we cannot, will not let them scare us. #25Jan
01:07:10 Jan 25

Gsquare86 Gigi Ibrahim جيجي
Tomorrow will be what we make it to be, so let's make it an
up-rise the police can't forget #Jan25
02:26:40 Jan 25

2

THE DAY OF REVOLT

...on which the Revolution starts

 TravellerW Mo-ha-med
Police throws rocks @ demonstrtrs while we raised our arms.
We're unarmed, they're in full gear. We are strong, they're
weak. #25jan #Egypt

TUESDAY, JANUARY 25, WAS National Police Day, a public holiday in Egypt, an appropriate date for protests. The call went out on Facebook and through social networks. There would be demonstrations across Egypt, including in Alexandria, Suez, and Cairo.

In the capital a loose strategy had been devised in meetings and online. The plan was for multiple fast-moving demonstrations in twenty locations around the city, designed to try to mobilize the people in poorer areas (who could not afford the luxury of computers and the internet) and avoid the usual police tactic of cordoning off protesters and preventing them from rallying.

The strategy was effective, but it was the sheer numbers who turned out that took the police by surprise. In the early afternoon the demonstrations started, ranging in strength from a few dozen to a few thousand. Protesters marched through the back streets in districts like Shubra and Boulaq, gathering people as they went, all the while tweeting news of their location and progress.

After several violent clashes with police the different marches converged in Midan Al-Tahrir (Liberation Square) in the center of the city. Overwhelming the police through force of numbers and courage, protesters occupied the Square despite tear gas, rock throwing, sticks and water cannon being used against them.

Taken aback by their success, once in Tahrir the activists had to work out what to do next. The social movements had a meeting. The initial idea was to call for the arrest of the Interior Minister, but the people in the Square, most of whom were not part of any political group, were chanting for the removal of the regime. The activists realized they could not call for less than the demonstrators wanted. So the demands of the Revolution were set by the spontaneous chants of the People.

After nightfall the police broke up the demonstration using rubber bullets and tear gas, and skirmishes continued into the early hours.

At one stage in the afternoon the Egyptian government had blocked Twitter. But the barrier of fear that had protected Hosni Mubarak's regime for thirty years had already been smashed to pieces.

monasosh monasosh
Praying wt tear gas around #jan25 http://yfrog.com/h2prdjj

3arabawy Hossam عمو حسام
streets r empty. Police r everywhere. #jan25
09:27:57 Jan 25

Gsquare86 Gigi Ibrahim جيجي
great start RT @3arabawy: streets r empty. Police r
everywhere. #jan25
09:28:26 Jan 25

Sandmonkey Mahmoud Salem
Shower, Crago pants, Hoodie, running shoes, phone charged,
cash, ID, cigs (for jail) and some mace just in case. Am ready!
#jan25
10:04:18 Jan 25

adamakary Adam Makary
#jan25 protester's demands: increase in minimum wage,
dismissal of interior ministry, removal of emergency law,
shorten presidential term
10:15:08 Jan 25

adamakary Adam Makary
#jan25 protests will take place all throughout cairo, including
shubra, mohendessin, in front of cairo university and on arab
league street
10:17:45 Jan 25

adamakary Adam Makary
lets not forget mp's loyal to mubarak have previously said
that protesters can be shot at if they pose a threat to national
security #jan25
10:23:12 Jan 25

ManarMohsen Manar Mohsen
Those tweeting about the protest in Egypt, please use the
hashtag #Jan25 in order to spread any information.
10:54:41 Jan 25

3arabawy Hossam عمو حسام
@shadihamid I'm not expecting a revolution today. I'm
expecting protests. So let's not shoot high so as not to
disappoint people later.
11:02:28 Jan 25

Sarahngb Sarahngb
Tahrir square looks scary. Cordons, policemen, fire trucks, CS trucks. #Jan25
11:38:28 Jan 25

norashalaby Nora Shalaby
It's really satisfying to c Egyptian police officers working & anxious on their day off #jan25
12:11:05 Jan 25

Gsquare86 Gigi Ibrahim جيجي
Don't let the police intimidate us with their presence, they always have been there and always will, it's time to move #Jan25
12:11:59 Jan 25

monasosh monasosh
Heading towards gam3et el dowal st, empowered #jan25 #nahya http://yfrog.com/gzljqeu

tarekshalaby Tarek Shalaby
Today's our day as #CitizenJournalists to cover and share the truth freely. Regardless of the outcome we are winners cuz we're a team #jan25
12:45:57 Jan 25

Sandmonkey Mahmoud Salem
Huge demo going to tahrir #jan25 shit just got real
13:21:56 Jan 25

ManarMohsen Manar Mohsen
Security presence in Tahrir is insane, protest from dar elgalaa
moved to tahrir square #Jan25
13:32:05 Jan 25

Sandmonkey Mahmoud Salem
Security tried to storm protestors. Failed. Regrouping. #jan25
13:33:38 Jan 25

norashalaby Nora Shalaby
Fuck got kettled almost suffocated till they broke cordon
13:42:54 Jan 25

ManarMohsen Manar Mohsen
Beating up protesters in kasr elnil. Protesters marching,
chanting "freedom" #jan25
13:45:05 Jan 25

monasosh monasosh
This is great, we r in nahya street, ppl r walking by our side
#jan25
13:56:06 Jan 25

norashalaby Nora Shalaby
Police trying to barricade but can't
14:02:39 Jan 25

Ghonim Wael Ghonim
Everyone come to Dar ElHekma security police allow people
to join us and we are few hundreds #Jan25
14:08:55 Jan 25

3arabawy Hossam عمو حسام
Protests have started in Alexandria http://english.ahram.org.
eg/News/4773.aspx #Jan25
14:10:14 Jan 25

mosaaberizing Mosa'ab Elshamy
Amazing scene at Mostafa Mahmoud. Thousands marching
with Egypt flag. #Jan25
14:22:03 Jan 25

Gsquare86 Gigi Ibrahim جيجي
I am looking at shubra's residents reaction from the balconies and they r chanting with us #jan25 http://yfrog.com/h29m5hrj
14:28:32 Jan 25

ManarMohsen Manar Mohsen
The main aim of the coordinators is to not get barricaded by security forces. #Jan25
14:29:45 Jan 25

ashrafkhalil ashraf khalil
#Jan25 grandma with maybe 4 teeth chanting along happily in boulaq as marchers pass
14:32:41 Jan 25

ashrafkhalil ashraf khalil
#Jan25 at the very least this is the biggest day of protests Egypt has seen in years
14:45:48 Jan 25

ashrafkhalil ashraf khalil
#Jan25 crowds overwhelming police cordons outside courthouse downtown!
14:50:17 Jan 25

monasosh monasosh
If u r not here, u r missing a lot. Down wt mobarak . Mohandesin #jan25
14:51:54 Jan 25

norashalaby Nora Shalaby
Trying to break the cordon in front of court #Jan 25
14:52:46 Jan 25

monasosh monasosh
I know this will sound corny, but I have never felt like this is my country more than now #jan25
14:54:48 Jan 25

TravellerW Mo-ha-med
our strength is in our collective action. Egyptians, Believe in Yourselves. BELIEVE IN US. #25jan #egypt
14:57:04 Jan 25

3arabawy Hossam عمو حسام
The chant in many of the protests is "إرحل" (LEAVE!) Just like #Tunisia. #jan25
14:58:00 Jan 25

ashrafkhalil ashraf khalil
#Jan25 the central security guys look miserable. Crowd making A major push against them. Happy Police Day guys!
14:58:00 Jan 25

tarekshalaby Tarek Shalaby
This is happening!!! #jan25 http://twitpic.com/3t9m00
15:00:29 Jan 25

Gsquare86 Gigi Ibrahim جيجي
Thugs all around us marching beside us #jan25 shubra http://yfrog.com/h5ybskj
15:00:46 Jan 25

adamakary Adam Makary
Ppl are stomping their feet, imitating sounds from a boot camp, now ppl stop for the call to prayer #jan25
15:06:16 Jan 25

tarekshalaby Tarek Shalaby
#A7A #A7A #A7A!!! This is fuckin happening! http://twitpic.com/3t9o3c
15:07:09 Jan 25

Ghonim Wael Ghonim
Protests are like watermelons and it seems I opened the wrong one #Frustrated #Jan25
15:08:50 Jan 25

TravellerW Mo-ha-med
#jan25 violence on the galaa bridge. W pushed through - but now we're stck on the bridge.
15:14:18 Jan 25

monasosh monasosh
Heading to kasr el nil bridge, massive crowd, there might be violence. Rabena yostor #jan25 http://yfrog.com/hsbjnxj
15:14:26 Jan 25

tarekshalaby Tarek Shalaby
Fuck! We're getting hit. Broke through 2 lines. No serious injuries #jan25
15:15:57 Jan 25

TravellerW Mo-ha-med
That was bad. Very vicious soliers and officers with batons
15:16:00 Jan 25

Gsquare86 Gigi Ibrahim جيجي
We are taking all the tight streets of shubra with us to Ramsesees we are heading #jan25 http://yfrog.com/h56kshgj
15:30:06 Jan 25

Salamander Sally Sami
The march from Mohandessin reached Tahrir square and a fire engine passed spraying water on protesters and left #jan25
15:40:41 Jan 25

ashrafkhalil ashraf khalil
#Jan25 crowd chanting ' salmeya' peaceful
15:40:47 Jan 25

3arabawy Hossam عمو حسام
Protesters in Shubra are trying to head to Tahrir Square.
Protesters in downtown Cairo climb firetruck and destroy
water cannon. #Jan25
15:43:34 Jan 25

Ghonim Wael Ghonim
We got brutally beaten up by police people #Jan25
15:46:29 Jan 25

Sandmonkey Mahmoud Salem
Police officer speaking on cellphone : "eiwa ya basha ,the gas
is on the way". Teargas is coming. #jan25
15:50:49 Jan 25

3arabawy Hossam عمو حسام
Sinai demonstrators continue their sit in blocking airport road.
Thousands r reportedly protesting in Zagazig & Suez http://bit.
ly/gn6Ss9
15:53:52 Jan 25

ashrafkhalil ashraf khalil
#Jan25 amazing! Huge crowd just rushed in from abdeen to
join thousands controlling half of tahrir square
15:57:42 Jan 25

norashalaby Nora Shalaby
Tear gas!!
15:58:37 Jan 25

TravellerW Mo-ha-med
tear gas #25jan
15:59:10 Jan 25

monasosh monasosh
Eyes burning fuck #jan25 http://yfrog.com/gy70kgj
16:00:04 Jan 25

norashalaby Nora Shalaby
Tear gas is fucking deadly. Cant see!
16:04:42 Jan 25

norashalaby Nora Shalaby
Ppl throwing us water bottles from Windows
16:09:09 Jan 25

norashalaby Nora Shalaby
Someone is hurt. Need a doctor
16:13:22 Jan 25

ashrafkhalil ashraf khalil
#Jan25 police and protestors in tahrir all gagging on tear gas
16:14:45 Jan 25

norashalaby Nora Shalaby
Water being shot at us. Protesters throwing rocks
16:18:54 Jan 25

ashrafkhalil ashraf khalil
#Jan25 crowd regrouping and now controls most of tahrir square
16:19:59 Jan 25

monasosh monasosh
Police is throwing rocks at us #jan25 http://yfrog.com/h06ipbj
16:21:43 Jan 25

monasosh monasosh
Someone badly injured in his leg #jan25
16:23:58 Jan 25

TravellerW Mo-ha-med
Police throws rocks @ demonstrtrs while we raised our arms. We're unarmed, they're in full gear. We are strong, they're weak. #25jan #Egypt
16:27:33 Jan 25

ashrafkhalil ashraf khalil
#Jan25 I will never get used to the sight of the riot police throwing rocks at protestors. Does that happen anywhere else?!
16:38:53 Jan 25

Ghonim Wael Ghonim
Everyone come to Tahrir now we need you we are no less than 10,000 and no more police #JAN25
16:42:32 Jan 25

monasosh monasosh
So far helped clean the wounds of 3. Many are injured minor injuries in their head from rocks #jan25
16:48:32 Jan 25

Ghonim Wael Ghonim
Come to Tahrir please #Jan25
16:59:14 Jan 25

TWITTER BLOCKED

3arabawy Hossam عمر حسام
Back on Twitter via Proxy. Fuck you hosni! #Jan25
18:34:18 Jan 25

3arabawy Hossam عمر حسام
Ya shabab, Tahrir is a war zone now. Tens of thousands r protesting the same chants as the Tunisians. #Jan25
18:34:52 Jan 25

Sarahngb Sarahngb
We have news of rubber bullets being fired in tahrir sq. and people are not budging. Infact, they are increasing in number #jan25
18:36:37 Jan 25

Sandmonkey Mahmoud Salem
Charging my phone and getting water and supplies to tahrir peeps. Do the same. Support ur people. #jan25
18:37:25 Jan 25

3arabawy Hossam عمر حسام
to break the block on Twitter use this proxy: http://hidemyass.com/ #Jan25
18:40:10 Jan 25

Sarahngb Sarahngb
amazing sight as masses were coming from every direction
towards tahrir square. It's the demo's meeting point. Amazing
#jan25
18:42:47 Jan 25

3arabawy Hossam عمرو حسام
Mubarak's posters in Alexandria destroyed! #Jan25 http://
is.gd/1OS8lt
18:54:10 Jan 25

Sarahngb Sarahngb
Its almost impossible to tweet or catch network. Come on!
Join us in tahreer sq. #jan25
20:35:41 Jan 25

monasosh monasosh
All telecommunications are down in tahrir square. We can't
call or update twitter. I went out to update u and get updates
#jan25
20:57:25 Jan 25

3arabawy Hossam عمرو حسام
What is everyone is almost sure about is that the police will
attack at some point, and not let the occupation continue till
tomorrow #Jan25
21:35:40 Jan 25

3arabawy Hossam عمرو حسام
Two protesters killed in Suez #Jan25 http://bit.ly/iiTLIP
21:47:02 Jan 25

Gsquare86 Gigi Ibrahim جيجي
OMG Twitter is back!! Thank god ! The situation in Tahrir is
beyond amazing eveeryone should head there #jan25
21:58:59 Jan 25

RamyYaacoub Ramy Yaacoub
RT @Sarahngb: Thousands of People still at tahrir square
chanting 'al sha3b yoreed esqat el nizam' 'the people want
the system down' #jan25
22:37:14 Jan 25

Ghonim Wael Ghonim
Egypt after #Jan25 is no way going to be the same as Egypt before it. Today we proved so many points.
00:45:14 Jan 26

3arabawy Hossam عمو حسام
Police has started attacking the downtown Cairo occupation. Reports of tear gas fired and arrests. Protesters chased to side roads. #Jan25
00:47:41 Jan 26

Sarahngb Sarahngb
Panic struck in tahrir square. Several ambulance cars #jan25
01:11:49 Jan 26

monasosh monasosh
We need doctors to head to hisham mobarak, 3 badly injured and we need help #jan25
01:18:25 Jan 26

Ghonim Wael Ghonim
Now in Tahrir situation is out of control. Prevented 2 angry guys from throwing a huge metal on police cars from top of the bridge! #Jan25
01:36:48 Jan 26

NevineZaki Nevine
I CAN NOT BELIEVE WHAT IT HAS REACHED TO, THIS IS INSANE! #JAN25
01:40:49 Jan 26

Gsquare86 Gigi Ibrahim جيجي
Tahrir got broken up by police using tear gas, rubber bullets, water hoses, & rock-throwing..ppl r still marching in DT #Jan25..I'm home
01:58:06 Jan 26

Salamander Sally Sami
From 6 october bridge security chasing protesters with tear gas and rubber bullets #25jan #jan25 #cairo
02:04:07 Jan 26

norashalaby Nora Shalaby
Just got home after being bombarded with dozen of tear gas canisters! What a day #jan 25
02:21:01 Jan 26

norashalaby Nora Shalaby
Those protesters that have remained in the streets despite the lastest police brutality against us are really really brave #jan
02:47:44 Jan 26

monasosh monasosh
One of the injured protesters went to hospital and was beaten up there! #jan25
02:48:36 Jan 26

3arabawy Hossam عمو حسام
New post: #Jan25 Police attack @ 1:20am, downtown Cairo
http://bit.ly/hSkLwZ
04:06:32 Jan 26

mosaaberizing Mosa'ab Elshamy
Probably need a blog post on it's own but I'll try noting some unforgettable moments/scenes from this day in the next tweets.. #jan25
04:15:28 Jan 26

mosaaberizing Mosa'ab Elshamy
1. Breaking 1st cordon at Qasr Elnil bridge was HUGE. Seeing the fuckers run away from us and open other cordons. Priceless feeling. #Jan25
04:22:33 Jan 26

mosaaberizing Mosa'ab Elshamy
2. People handshaking, hugging & offering flowers to officers. Same protesters who later refused beating an isolated soldier. Classy. #Jan25
04:32:26 Jan 26

mosaaberizing Mosa'ab Elshamy
3. A family I met - young couple with their 2 yrs old son - came all the way from Alex to Tahrir and wanted to stay all night. #Jan25
04:40:02 Jan 26

mosaaberizing Mosa'ab Elshamy
4. People burning up a CSF car in rage after the last attack on Tahrir. Those inside of it were weeping for mercy. #Jan25
04:44:40 Jan 26

mosaaberizing Mosa'ab Elshamy
5. Crippled guy on chair wheel protesting. A blind one too with stick. Let me hear anyone talking shit ever again about this nation.. #Jan25
04:57:28 Jan 26

mosaaberizing Mosa'ab Elshamy
Everyone cried at some point. If the amazing scenes and emotions weren't touching enough for some, the tear gas took care of that. #Jan25
05:28:01 Jan 26

monasosh monasosh
I know this is silly but my foot really hurts @alaa @manal & @RamyRaoof not here I feel like crying
05:35:13 Jan 26

monasosh monasosh
#Jan25 I was there today, tomorrow YOU SHOULD BE WT US http://yfrog.com/static/images/logo.gif
05:41:08 Jan 26

monasosh monasosh
All injured protesters who went to hospital were turned in to the police (via @malek) #Jan25
05:43:29 Jan 26

TravellerW Mo-ha-med
Exhausted. Will catch a few hours of sleep. Good morning, Egypt. #25jan
07:17:28 Jan 26

TravellerW Mo-ha-med
Quick update on last night, 1am: attacks by tear gas - a dozen a minute, which is INSANE - followed by armed gov thugs attacks. #25jan
07:23:53 Jan 26

Photograph by @sarahcarr Sarah Carr - www.inanities.org

3

WEDNESDAY, JANUARY 26
KEEPING THE STREETS UNSETTLED

...as protests continue throughout Egypt

 Packafy Pakinam Ahmed
after 2 days of protesting , tear gas is like fresh air , rubber
bullets are like rain drops , sticks r like thai massage ....

KEEN TO DEMONSTRATE that the remarkable success of January 25 was not a one-off, activists in Cairo continued to protest, although on a working day numbers were far smaller. The police, smarting from the day before, responded with brutal force.

The government blocked Facebook, but not before the We Are All Khaled Said page had put out a call for mass demonstrations to take place on Friday.

Meanwhile the revolt in other parts of Egypt deepened. There were incredibly violent scenes in the port town of Suez, where several protesters were killed as they drove the police back.

At 10:00 pm, Wael Ghonim, the head of marketing for Google in the Middle East and North Africa, appeared on a popular Egyptian TV talk show to denounce internet censorship. He would appear again on the show twelve days later, but in very different circumstances.

Sandmonkey Mahmoud Salem
Please remember, it took a month of protests 4 Tunis
revolution 2 succeed. Persistence is everything #jan25
10:27:35 Jan 26

Gsquare86 Gigi Ibrahim جيجي
anyone knows what is going on today.when and where?
#Jan25
12:32:09 Jan 26

Zeinobia Zeinobia
I have a confession : I did not think for one second that
#Jan25 would be so great like that
13:08:54 Jan 26

3arabawy Hossam عمرو حسام
200 detainees from yesterday r kept at State Security Police
HQ in Nasr City (via @Malek) #Jan25 SS police is Mubarak's
gestapo.
13:33:35 Jan 26

Zeinobia Zeinobia
There are clashes in Madinet Nasr between the security
forces and protesters , the people are helping the protesters
#Jan25
13:46:00 Jan 26

ashrafkhalil ashraf khalil
#Jan25 trapped with cynical cab driver "this won't produce
anything. It's too late for us. Tunisia is different, they're more
advanced"
14:09:01 Jan 26

monasosh monasosh
I am thinking swimming goggles in the next demo againt tear
gas #Jan25
14:32:36 Jan 26

Sandmonkey Mahmoud Salem
We r at the press syndicate. 200+ and growing. Come join us
now. #jan25
15:00:19 Jan 26

3arabawy Hossam عمو حسام
Facebook it seems has been blocked in Egypt! #Jan25 I can't log into my account. Other friends r reporting the same.
15:17:57 Jan 26

Ghonim Wael Ghonim
The Egyptian government started to take really stupid actions that will result in nothing but encouraging more people to protest #Jan25
15:19:14 Jan 26

ManarMohsen Manar Mohsen
From Khaled Said group: Mass protests are scheduled after Friday prayers all over Egypt. Please spread the word. #Jan25 #Egypt
15:23:40 Jan 26

HosniMobarak Hosni Mobarak
I blocked Twitter and Facebook so you could focus on your work, not run around the streets shouting. #jan25
15:54:19 Jan 26

Sandmonkey Mahmoud Salem
The crowd got dispersed. Heading to greener pastures. We r isolated. U can hear women screaming. #jan25
16:11:04 Jan 26

monasosh monasosh
Right now infront of my eyes, tear gas, they beat protestors and arrested some #Jan25
16:25:51 Jan 26

Ghonim Wael Ghonim
To all Egyptians silence is a crime now! #Jan25
17:18:09 Jan 26

3arabawy Hossam عمو حسام
I called my internet service provider. They confirmed Facebook and Twitter r blocked by the govt. #Jan25
17:19:12 Jan 26

mosaaberizing Mosa'ab Elshamy
Live bullets? FUCK YOU MUBARAK!!
17:19:27 Jan 26

ManarMohsen Manar Mohsen
Very violent at Galaa street under the 26 July Bridge and 15
May Bridge. Security forces are on one side and protests on
another. #Jan2
17:28:25 Jan 26

ManarMohsen Manar Mohsen
Hundreds are running into the streets because the security
forces started to suddenly beat them with sticks. Observers
and protesters #Jan25
17:52:21 Jan 26

ManarMohsen Manar Mohsen
Galaa st. just turned into a war zone. I saw over 100 security
forces join those already in Ramsees & beat everyone without
exception #Jan25
18:05:00 Jan 26

Gsquare86 Gigi Ibrahim جيجي
Beating and shootings on Ramses streets for no fuckin
reason!
18:17:28 Jan 26

Gsquare86 Gigi Ibrahim جيجي
Tahrir square has unbelievable amount of security I am
worried to take out my phone to take a picture I would get
arrested #jan25
18:32:13 Jan 26

monasosh monasosh
More organized protests will be held Friday, but from now till
then help us make the streets unsettle #Jan25
18:38:44 Jan 26

Zeinobia Zeinobia
Huge clashes in Suez city , people remember this could be
our #Sidibouzid
19:08:31 Jan 26

mosaaberizing Mosa'ab Elshamy
Tahrir sq. never looks the same anymore, now that it's back to
"normal". Can't wait till Friday. #Jan25
20:02:57 Jan 26

Ghonim Wael Ghonim
I'm going to be talking today to Mona ElShazly about #Jan25
and Internet censorship.
20:26:51 Jan 26

3arabawy Hossam عمرو حسام
NDP offices and police stations are attacked and burned
down by protesters in Suez, says Al-Jazeera. #Jan25
22:09:14 Jan 26

MennaAmr Menna Amr
Baradei to join protesters on Friday. Too good to be true?
http://bit.ly/gzPt4o
22:31:24 Jan 26

3arabawy Hossam عمرو حسام
There r calls circulating widely via SMS for protests on Friday
following the prayers. #Jan25
22:40:07 Jan 26

ashrafkhalil ashraf khalil
#Jan25 amazing details coming out of suez! Seems like an
absolute war zone. Are there any pix or video that anyone
knows about?
22:47:18 Jan 26

mosaaberizing Mosa'ab Elshamy
Finally home. Almost got arrested at Tahrir but fought back &
ran away. Got some hits and lost my phone & a camera in the
process. #Jan25
22:57:32 Jan 26

Zeinobia Zeinobia
Violent clashes between protesters and security forces at the
ministry of foreign affairs building in Cairo #Jan25
23:32:26 Jan 26

Sandmonkey Mahmoud Salem
The revolt continues. Egypt won't stop, won't give in. This isn't
a one day event. It's a wave. It won't stop. #jan25
23:41:29 Jan 26

Ghonim Wael Ghonim
I tried to stay balanced on 10pm with Mona ElShazly but I
couldn't its time to be biased towards the people's choice in
Egypt. #Jan25
00:18:53 Jan 27

HosniMobarak Hosni Mobarak
Habib just sent me a bbm. He says I should prepare a farewell speech for my citizens. Where are you guys going? #jan25
01:31:38 Jan 27

Packafy Pakinam Ahmed
Via facebook : Mostafa Al Faramawy: ...
02:02:42 Jan 27

Packafy Pakinam Ahmed
after 2 days of protesting , tear gas is like fresh air , rubber bullets are like rain drops , sticks r like thai massage ....
02:03:06 Jan 27

Gsquare86 Gigi Ibrahim جيجي
I have one of those on my back..it still hurts http://yfrog.com/h290794515j #EgyPolice #Jan25 down with pigs!
03:42:58 Jan 27

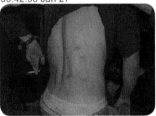

justicentric justicentric
Video: Egypt- Demonstrators refuse to leave rails of metro while train tries to move anyway http://ow.ly/3KXWi #JAN25
03:53:58 Jan 27

Gsquare86 Gigi Ibrahim جيجي
revolution is keeping me sleepless thinking, anticipating, dreaming, and reflecting, i want to wake up to a better and free #Egypt
04:31:49 Jan 27

4

ANTICIPATION

...as Egypt braces itself

Ghonim Wael Ghonim
Pray for #Egypt. Very worried as it seems that government is planning a war crime tomorrow against people. We are all ready to die #Jan25

WHILE BATTLES RAGED for a third day in Suez, in Cairo the streets were tense. Air that had been filled with tear gas was now thick with anticipation for the planned demonstration on Friday, which protesters, still coming to terms with the shock of their success on January 25, expected to be huge.

Not all would be able to take part, as around 1,000 people had already been imprisoned since protests began. Joining them on Thursday night was Wael Ghonim, the Google employee, who subsequently disappeared without trace.

Western media attention was focused on two forces: the Muslim Brotherhood and Mohamed ElBaradei. The Muslim Brotherhood, Egypt's largest established (although banned) opposition group, had previously decided not to support the January 25 demonstration. It now changed its position for the Friday protest, but it was not leading events on the ground.

Mohamed ElBaradei, the former UN nuclear inspector seen by many as a future presidential candidate, flew into Cairo in the evening. At the airport, as in the streets, he found that the protesters were not waiting for him.

ashrafkhalil ashraf khalil
#Jan25 couple thoughts to start day: outsiders need to know that all this is happening independent of the Muslim Brotherhood! That's amazing
08:13:31 Jan 27

ashrafkhalil ashraf khalil
#Jan25 thought #2: the central security guys must be exhausted by now. This is more than what they trained for and protestors know it!
08:16:04 Jan 27

ashrafkhalil ashraf khalil
#Jan25 thought no. 3: the people of suez are absolute bad-asses. The canal cities have always been tough and defiant
08:19:12 Jan 27

Sandmonkey Mahmoud Salem
No one can sleep, even though everyone is tired. We all need our rest, but who can really rest in such days? #jan25
09:26:41 Jan 27

Sandmonkey Mahmoud Salem
Whatever the outcome, whatever ur position, go out & join ur countrymen. These are the moments where history gets made.Be part of it. #jan25
09:28:39 Jan 27

Sarahngb Sarahngb
Everyone on twitter, Egyptian or not, supporting Egypt and #jan25 is part of the reason why we're trending, why the world noticed...
11:32:38 Jan 27

Gsquare86 Gigi Ibrahim جيجي
Today is Khaled Said's birthday. We all have to go in the streets tomorrow so his blood doesn't go in vain #Jan25 #AntiTorture #FreeEgypt
11:55:04 Jan 27

Sandmonkey Mahmoud Salem
Screw this. We don't need leaders! " Al Arabiya: Elbaradei says ready to 'lead the transition' in Egypt http://bit.ly/dWMcwO #jan25"
15:28:58 Jan 27

Sarahcarr أبو كار
Send your thoughts to Suez whose brave people are currently at war with the police for a third day. Reports of live ammunition being used
15:52:30 Jan 27

Gsquare86 Gigi Ibrahim جيجي
I am in ramsis !!! Nothing is happening!!!! Just security and people selling things on streets #Jan25
16:11:56 Jan 27

Egyptocracy Egyptocracy
Told my mother I will be on the street on Friday and she didn't try to stop me as usual. #Egypt #Jan25
16:16:07 Jan 27

3arabawy Hossam عمو حسام
shop owners in the neighborhood r excited about tomorrow's protest. Laundry workers will join #jan25
16:21:07 Jan 27

3arabawy Hossam عمو حسام
friend called to say 2 of her friends will protest tomorrow. The couple work as investment bankers! Mubarak managed to alienate all classes.
18:25:21 Jan 27

3arabawy Hossam عمو حسام
People around the world, plz picket #Egypt embassies tomorrow Friday in solidarity. #Jan25
18:26:25 Jan 27

Sandmonkey Mahmoud Salem
The egyptian football league cancelled. Funfact: next game is between elahly and the police team. Highly political shit. #jan25
18:40:26 Jan 27

Sandmonkey Mahmoud Salem
This is becoming the region first telecommunication civil war. Our internet & smart phones are weapons they won't allow us to have. #jan25
18:44:54 Jan 27

Gsquare86 Gigi Ibrahim حبيبج
I am sure Egypt will rise up tomorrow on a Friday just like
Tunisia did on a Friday also! #Jan25 #FreeEgypt
20:41:15 Jan 27

3arabawy Hossam عمو حسام
Sinai Bedouins use RPG against police in Sinai. Welcome to
the revolution. http://is.gd/VZVa9N #Jan25
20:41:40 Jan 27

ManarMohsen Manar Mohsen
One of the best things about this uprising is that it's from and
for the people, not the parties, not ElBaradei. Keep it that way.
#Jan25
21:45:44 Jan 27

ashrafkhalil ashraf khalil
#Jan25 El Baradei told me in Dec. he'd be willing to take to
the streets if he knew he'd have huge numbers behind him.
Seems that day is here
21:55:43 Jan 27

ashrafkhalil ashraf khalil
#Jan25 but worth noting that the protesters aren't begging for
ElBaradei to come save them. This happened without him
21:57:37 Jan 27

ManarMohsen Manar Mohsen
Let's face it. Even if tomorrow fails, the movement will make
another #Jan25, another Friday, another Facebook event.
There's no going back.
22:44:11 Jan 27

ManarMohsen Manar Mohsen
Word is that there will be a shutdown on all forms of
communications, and that Cairo will be completely blockaded
for tomorrow. #Jan25
23:02:54 Jan 27

3arabawy Hossam عمو حسام
No one knows what tomorrow is gonna be like. But I'm very
hopeful. I'm very optimistic Mubarak's reign is about to end.
#Jan25 #revolution
23:04:17 Jan 27

monasosh monasosh
Just convinced a taxi driver to join the demonstrations
tomorrow yaaaaay #Jan25
23:30:55 Jan 27

MohammedY Mohammed Yahia
@gregbranch I keep hoping this will spread to more and more
countries. I'm sick of waiting for democracy from the West, its
time we TAKE IT!
23:47:29 Jan 27

Gsquare86 Gigi Ibrahim جيجي
You can strike me with a bullet, but you can't take away my
dignity #EgyPolice #Mubarak #Egypt #Jan25
00:05:42 Jan 28

Ghonim Wael Ghonim
Pray for #Egypt. Very worried as it seems that government
is planning a war crime tomorrow against people. We are all
ready to die #Jan25
00:07:04 Jan 28

5

FRIDAY, JANUARY 28
The Day of Rage

...on which the protesters defeat the police and Egypt catches fire

SHORTLY AFTER MIDNIGHT on January 28, Egypt went offline. In an unprecedented action the Egyptian government ordered internet service providers and mobile phone operators to shut down. Terrified of the new tools of Twitter and Facebook, and the uncensored visual media of yFrog, Flickr and YouTube, the regime chose to pay the price of millions of lost dollars to the economy in order to deprive protesters of a key weapon – the means of communication. Only one ISP was exempted to enable the Egyptian stock exchange to stay connected.

It was futile. The Egyptian uprising had started online but on January 25 it had become something much bigger. Thousands of mostly young people had been confronted by the full force of the state for the first time, and were now in the street demanding the removal of the regime.

This was the bloodiest and most decisive day of the Revolution. There were demonstrations and fierce confrontations across the country, but the most iconic images came from Cairo.

The numbers were far greater than Tuesday. Hundreds of thousands poured onto the streets after Friday prayers, again flooding the residential districts and heading to the city center. Many came out of their apartments to join the protest as the marchers passed by.

The police responded immediately with water cannons and countless volleys of tear gas, often fired directly into crowds. "Thugs," violent men paid by the regime to inflict the worst brutality (an old tactic of Mubarak's) passed through police lines to attack protesters.

But they lost. In a key moment, on Kasr Al-Nil bridge police trying to prevent protesters reaching Tahrir Square were overwhelmed. They turned and ran. The battles continued as rubber bullets and live fire were used. But the hunters had become the hunted as protesters chased down Central Security Force (CSF) vans and torched them. The headquarters of the NDP, Hosni Mubarak's ruling party, was set on fire and black smoke billowed over Cairo as it burned to a shell.

By nightfall protesters had control of Tahrir Square, but had paid a heavy price. Hundreds were killed across Egypt, with most of the victims in Cairo. The dead included children, women, and the disabled. The most common causes of death were from gunfire, rubber bullets, and tear gas canisters fired at close range.

The government withdrew the police from the streets. Hosni Mubarak's security forces had been defeated. After dark, army tanks rolled into central Cairo but did not attempt to clear the demonstrators. A curfew was announced, and immediately ignored.

Mubarak appeared on state TV late at night to declare that he had dismissed his entire cabinet and would swear in a new government – but he would stay as president.

International reaction was mainly equivocal, calling for restraint on both sides and refusing to condemn Mubarak's regime. President Obama merely said he had urged Mubarak to "give meaning" to words of reform.

Due to the dearth of tweets caused by the internet blackout, this day is here represented by two black pages.

Photograph by @TravellerW Mohamed Al-Rahhal - www.travellerwithin.com

6

THE VANISHING STATE

...on which the police are absent, the Army is passive and the people take security into their own hands

Sandmonkey Mahmoud Salem
there's no state at the moment, we're governing ourselves
#Jan25

DESPITE THE BLOCKED INTERNET (*Egypt would remain cut off for a further four days*) *some activists managed to get online to report the news, either by phoning their tweets to friends abroad via landlines, finding a connection through the one remaining ISP used by the Egyptian stock exchange, or borrowing the satellite links of the international media.*

The regime was banking that the chaos caused by the removal of the police from the streets would terrify residents into begging the government to restore order. There were instances of looting and crime. But people's response was to form neighborhood groups to defend their streets and homes themselves.

The key question for the demonstrators was what the army would do. It was supposed to enforce the curfew, but made no serious attempt to do so. Protesters handed flowers and oranges to soldiers and implored them to come onto the side of the People.

Some security forces had barricaded themselves in the Interior Ministry. There were fatal clashes as they fired live ammunition at protesters trying to storm the building.

Meanwhile, Hosni Mubarak appointed his intelligence chief Omar Suleiman as his first ever vice president.

beleidy Amr El Beleidy
Good Morning! A new day, a new cabinet, come on let's hear
it, who's ruling us today? #Jan25
08:14:25 Jan 29

beleidy Amr El Beleidy
There is ZERO police presence, and saw two army vehicles
on the street, they're just sitting there #Jan25
10:01:25 Jan 29

beleidy Amr El Beleidy
Word of mouth on street: The police has completely
withdrawn under orders, when crime starts taking place ppl
will ask for them back #Jan25
12:56:06 Jan 29

Photograph by @3arabawy Hossam el-Hamalawy - www.arabawy.org

Sandmonkey Mahmoud Salem
Yesterday: we started protest in Imbaba w/10 ppl, grew to
10,000. Headed frm Imbaba 2 Mohandesin where police fired
tear gas #Jan25 (cont.)
13:31:35 Jan 29

Sandmonkey Mahmoud Salem
(cont.) joined by thousands in Mohandesin &headed to Dokki
trying 2 reach Tahrir. We were peaceful, it wasn't muslim
brotherhood #Jan25
13:32:38 Jan 29

Sandmonkey Mahmoud Salem
On Cobri Al-Jala2 there were two armored trucks destroyed.
On Cobri Qasr Al-Nil tear gas and shooting rubber bullets at
ppl #Jan25 #Egypt
13:37:13 Jan 29

Sandmonkey Mahmoud Salem
my friend Rashid &I were wearing gas masks &gloves so we
grabbed canisters &threw them away. I almost fainted frm tear
gas (cont.) #Jan25
13:39:11 Jan 29

Sandmonkey Mahmoud Salem
(cont.) when my friend tried 2 help me he got shot by rubber
bullets #Jan25 #Egypt
13:39:34 Jan 29

Sandmonkey Mahmoud Salem
NDP building burnt, police trucks burnt, graffiti against regime
in Ramsis and everywhere #Jan25 #Egypt
13:42:18 Jan 29

Gsquare86 Gigi Ibrahim جيجي
I have internet access from an 'unknown' location, the
people are in MILLIONS in the streets and will NOT stop until
MUBARAK is OUT!
13:45:09 Jan 29

Gsquare86 Gigi Ibrahim جيجي
i don't have net access for long, but all i want to say ...I AM
SOO PROUD OF BEING EGYPTIAN
13:46:43 Jan 29

Egypt is Free
Photograph by @3arabawy Hossam el-Hamalawy - www.arabawy.org

 Gsquare86 Gigi Ibrahim جيجي
The government have blocked everything because they are
soo afraid, but the people are not and will not give up!!
13:47:53 Jan 29

 Gsquare86 Gigi Ibrahim جيجي
so many people have died, hospitals are in need of blood,
please tell everyone u know to donate blood at hospitals
13:48:41 Jan 29

 Gsquare86 Gigi Ibrahim جيجي
the riot police was shooting at us with shrapnel bullets, live
bullets, water canon, rocks, and of course TEARGAS..
13:50:29 Jan 29

 Gsquare86 Gigi Ibrahim جيجي
IT WAS RAINING U.S.-MADE TEARGAS ON PEACEFUL
EGYPTIAN PROTESTERS CUZ THEY'RE DEMANDING
DIGINITY, JUSTICE,& FREEDOM MR.OBAMA, R U
LISTENING?
13:53:38 Jan 29

 Gsquare86 Gigi Ibrahim جيجي
Egyptian State-owned media is showing nothing from whatr's
really happening and trying to minimize it, BUT IT IS SOOOO
HUGE!
13:56:52 Jan 29

Gsquare86 Gigi Ibrahim جيجي
Demands are:1) MUBARAK OUT! 2)Dissmisal of gov &
parliament 3)Provisional government until free and fair
elections >>4m the Egyptian People!
13:59:16 Jan 29

 Gsquare86 Gigi Ibrahim جيجي
will the army be with the people? I think they will never shoot
at the people, they are there only to protect ..the police is out
14:28:17 Jan 29

 ashrafkhalil ashraf khalil
#jan25 Back online again for a bit thanks to the good folks at
BBC. Bunch of random observations to follow
15:45:06 Jan 29

 ashrafkhalil ashraf khalil
#jan25 Curfew starts in 15 minutes. No chance at all that the
protestors will obey. So the question becomes what will army
do after that?
15:47:30 Jan 29

The End
Photograph by @3arabawy Hossam el-Hamalawy - www.arabawy.org

ashrafkhalil ashraf khalil
#jan25 Was in Tahrir 10 minutes after Mubarak gave his
speech. Protestors though it was comical. They weren't even
mad, just laughed it off
15:55:34 Jan 29

sharifkouddous Sharif Kouddous
It's curfew. People are not leaving. They say the army won't
open fire. But there are some sounds of gunfire. #Egypt
16:02:48 Jan 29

beleidy Amr El Beleidy
The curfew has now been in effect for 10 mins, and nothing!
#Jan25
16:07:41 Jan 29

sharifkouddous Sharif Kouddous
I have never seen #Egypt this way. This is not Mubarak's
Egypt anymore. And it never will be again.
16: 09:37 Jan 29

ashrafkhalil ashraf khalil
#Jan25 Elements of self-policing on display. Saw volunteers
directing traffic at several intersections
16:16:58 Jan 29

NDP and Supreme Council of Press burnt down by protesters
Photograph by @3arabawy Hossam el-Hamalawy - www.arabawy.org

sharifkouddous Sharif Kouddous
People asking how I'm tweeting from Egypt, we are using a
work-around. Internet is still down and I can't send pics
16:23:44 Jan 29

sharifkouddous Sharif Kouddous
In the background of Tahrir, smoke rises from the burnt out
NDP party headquarters #Egypt
16:43:14 Jan 29

monasosh monasosh
Popular committees now r being formed in Alex & Cairo to
protect public & private properties from thugs #Jan25
16:43:33 Jan 29

sharifkouddous Sharif Kouddous
The police holed up in interior ministry are firing. Three people
bloodied carried out. The army is not shooting. #Egypt
17:01:41 Jan 29

sharifkouddous Sharif Kouddous
Amazing scene: three tanks roll by with a crowd of people
riding atop each one. Chanting 'Hosni Mubarak out!' #Egypt
17:15:32 Jan 29

The Battle for Lazoughli Square
Photograph by @3arabawy Hossam el-Hamalawy - www.arabawy.org

beleidy Amr El Beleidy
Omar Soleiman has been appointed vice-president Egypt #Jan25
17:18:23 Jan 29

ashrafkhalil ashraf khalil
#jan25 Trying to decide if Omar Suleiman as VP is meant to reassure the Egy people or the American govt. Washington does like and trust him
17:36:06 Jan 29

sharifkouddous Sharif Kouddous
There's not one policeman to be seen in Cairo. Some worried it's Mubarak's strategy to let people loot & burn. #Egypt
17:43:27 Jan 29

monasosh monasosh
Mobarak doesn't get atall what is happening in the street! WE DO NOT WANT YOU OR YOUR PPL! FUCK OFF! #Jan25
17:54:13 Jan 29

Sandmonkey Mahmoud Salem
In Heliopolis, police dressed as civilians r shooting gun fire to scare ppl. We're going out with sticks to ambush the thugs. #Jan25 #Egypt
17:54:18 Jan 29

monasosh monasosh
I am concerned,coz ppl r now leaving demo to go protect their places against thugs,But I am sure ppl won't settle till Mobarak leaves #Jan25
17:58:51 Jan 29

sharifkouddous Sharif Kouddous
Everyone talks about Friday like a war they won. 'Despite tear gas & beatings we just kept coming. We gave each other courage.' #Egypt
18:01:15 Jan 29

monasosh monasosh
Correction:only hundreds r reported to leave the demo,there r still more than 70000 demonstrator in Tahrir chanting agnst Mobarak #Jan25
18:08:42 Jan 29

Tahrir Square
Photograph by @3arabawy Hossam el-Hamalawy - www.arabawy.org

monasosh monasosh
Now they r chanting against Omar Sliman as well #Jan25
18:10:09 Jan 29

Sandmonkey Mahmoud Salem
street war in action. On nuzha street with 200 people
protecting the streets from drive-by shooters. It's same all
over Cairo #Jan25
18:22:14 Jan 29

Sandmonkey Mahmoud Salem
Police stations are empty, no police there #Jan25 #Egypt
18:22:36 Jan 29

Sandmonkey Mahmoud Salem
there's no state at the moment, we're governing ourselves
#Jan25
18:23:27 Jan 29

Sandmonkey Mahmoud Salem
no internet in Egypt. Calling in tweets to a friend in #Jordan
#Jan25 #Egypt
18:24:47 Jan 29

monasosh monasosh
Ppl r panicking, but ppl r managing to protect one another! #Jan25
19:03:51 Jan 29

Sandmonkey Mahmoud Salem
women carry sticks &join volunteer protection committees on the streets of Heliopolis. Ppl saluting army. It's great. #Jan25
19:37:22 Jan 29

beleidy Amr El Beleidy
Just ran in panic to the street as I heard a warning horn sound, it was a false alarm #Jan25
20:14:02 Jan 29

beleidy Amr El Beleidy
I'm feeling better now after seeing the response of the people on the street and their weapons #Jan25
20:15:11 Jan 29

ashrafkhalil ashraf khalil
#Jan25 Just talked with members of a large vigilante militia that set up a barricade on the corniche in Agouza
21:41:32 Jan 29

ashrafkhalil ashraf khalil
#Jan25 Crazy array of weapons on display with the militia. Lots of sticks and clubs, a weightifting bar, a machete and a field hockey stick
21:43:09 Jan 29

ashrafkhalil ashraf khalil
#Jan25 Militia outside is checking ID CARDSon everyone driving by. If you're not from the area, you need to have a good reason to be here
21:52:51 Jan 29

ashrafkhalil ashraf khalil
#Jan25 militia guys also said they reserve right to refuse you entry to the area if they simply don't like the look of you. Fair enough...
21:53:43 Jan 29

Sandmonkey Mahmoud Salem
ppl in neighborhoods wearing white bands to identify each
other #jan25
21:59:50 Jan 29

ashrafkhalil ashraf khalil
Militia guy: 'We don't need Mubarak. We don't need the army
or the police to protect us. This is the Egyptian people.'
22:00:09 Jan 29

ashrafkhalil ashraf khalil
#Jan25 Ther militia outside is a fairly motley and scary bunch.
Hate to be on their bad side but I DO feel safer with them
there
22:05:42 Jan 29

monasosh monasosh
PPl r calling 2 tell me that the situation is calmer in many
neighbouroods. Really all it need is for us to organize things
within us #Jan25
22:19:21 Jan 29

beleidy Amr El Beleidy
Sunrise is in 5 hours and 15 minutes, until then everyone will
be tense
01:34:42 Jan 30

beleidy Amr El Beleidy
I've become so tense any sound anywhere attracts my
attention, ppl on floor above me walking or moving stuff
doesn't help
01:43:10 Jan 30

beleidy Amr El Beleidy
Ok so people on our street have guns, that's better than sticks
02:18:30 Jan 30

beleidy Amr El Beleidy
Trying to figure out whether a perceived danger is real or just
in your head is a difficult thing
03:04:05 Jan 30

beleidy Amr El Beleidy
OK so I figure sources of worry are sensational TV reporting and emotional phone calls, complimented by stories from friends
03:22:32 Jan 30

monasosh monasosh
Recieved a message from Mobinil on behalf of the army urging ppl to to face thugs & protect the country,noting that WE cant send sms #Jan25
04:13:55 Jan 30

monasosh monasosh
Uploaded more videos http://tinyurl.com/657aemg extremely exhausted, everyone around is stealing couple of hrs sleep preparing 4 tom #Jan25
04:52:59 Jan 30

beleidy Amr El Beleidy
So things have been calm for a long time now, no gunshots, no friends calling with stories, light is in 45 minutes, a good time to sleep
04:53:26 Jan 30

7

NOT INTIMIDATED

...as the regime's efforts to restore fear are rebuffed

norashalaby Nora Shalaby
egyptian residents sweeping the streets and keeping order in
neighborhoods, mubarak's strategy not working! #jan25

*THERE WAS UNEASE in the Square. Protesters were unsure of the role of
the army, which had increased its presence on the streets. Hosni Mubarak
visited his military chiefs in a bid to shore up his power.*

*The curfew continued to be flouted, despite a deafening flyover by F-16
fighter jets on the curfew hour.*

Sandmonkey Mahmoud Salem
army tanks everywhere, stability nominally returned #jan25
11:20:26 Jan 30

Sandmonkey Mahmoud Salem
army was saluting volunteer protection groups on the street,
saying proud of them #jan25
11:24:19 Jan 30

Sandmonkey Mahmoud Salem
if ppl see a police officer on the street they'll probably beat
him up #jan25
11:29:21 Jan 30

monasosh monasosh
Back! woke up on the news that Egyptian gove issued an
order to shut down Aljazeera office here and withdraw permits
#Jan25
11:33:02 Jan 30

monasosh monasosh
I can feel it, it is so close my heart is racing, Mobarak is going
down #Jan25
14:15:45 Jan 30

Tahrir Square
Photograph by @3arabawy Hossam el-Hamalawy - www.arabawy.org

monasosh monasosh
I am heading 2 Tahrir sq,wt @RamyRaoof to join in the
protest, & drop medical supplies urgently needed to treat
wounded demonstrators #Jan25
14:28:18 Jan 30

Sandmonkey Mahmoud Salem
in tahrir now, everyone here, ppl of ALL classes, army letting
us in, v peaceful #jan25
14:28:26 Jan 30

beleidy Amr El Beleidy
Tahrir Square is happening! People are gathering there,
morale is high, army is friendly and letting people in #Jan25
Egypt
14:46:56 Jan 30

beleidy Amr El Beleidy
There were chants: The Army and the people are one hand,
and Peaceful Peaceful! Tahrir Square #Jan25 Egypt
14:54:33 Jan 30

3arabawy Hossam عمو حسام
I managed to get internet access for few mins.. All MSM
reports about looting, violence r EXAGGERATED! Protests r
still going on strong.
15:02:49 Jan 30

3arabawy Hossam عمو حسام
There r tens of thousands continuing the protests day and
night in Tahrir Sq. Yesterday we almost stormed the Interior
Ministry.
15:03:30 Jan 30

3arabawy Hossam عمو حسام
The police has vanished from the streets. They r barricaded
inside their Interior Ministry, stationing snipers on buildings,
shooting at us.
15:04:10 Jan 30

3arabawy Hossam عمو حسام
Live ammunition was used yesterday against us in Mohamed
Mahmoud Street. I saw at least one person dead.
15:05:06 Jan 30

Gsquare86 Gigi Ibrahim جيجي
So many are dead by live amo at the interior ministry in Cairo
by police
15:05:31 Jan 30

3arabawy Hossam عمو حسام
I'm ok, I have sustained injuries like everyone else from BB
bullets and rubber bullets. But my family and I are fine.
15:05:41 Jan 30

Gsquare86 Gigi Ibrahim جيجي
The Egyptian people WILL NOT STOP until Mubarak is OUT!!
the protests are only increasing in number and media is lying
15:06:16 Jan 30

Gsquare86 Gigi Ibrahim جيجي
The sit-in in Tahrir is on going and will not stop until Mubarak
is out! it is not shrinking either, it is only getting stronger!!
15:11:22 Jan 30

3arabawy Hossam عمو حسام
My neighborhood Nasr City, my city Cairo and in all Egyptian
towns, popular committees r being formed by citizens to
provide security.
15:11:24 Jan 30

3arabawy Hossam عمو حسام
Barricades r up, cars r checked by the shabab. Saboteurs r
beaten up immediately on the spot.
15:12:02 Jan 30

3arabawy Hossam عمو حسام
The shootings around Lazoughli and the snipers firing at
protesters yesterday happened as the army sat and watch.
15:13:15 Jan 30

3arabawy Hossam عمو حسام
WE DO NOT WANT THE ARMY! THE ARMY HAS BEEN
RULING SINCE 1952. THEY R NOT NEUTRAL PLAYERS.
15:13:40 Jan 30

3arabawy Hossam عمو حسام
The curfew the army imposed is meaningless. We break it every night by continuing our protests in Tahrir.
15:14:19 Jan 30

3arabawy Hossam عمو حسام
It is not true what some MSM outlets r broadcasting about the Muslim Brotherhood and the 6th of April leading the protests. It's complete BS
15:16:02 Jan 30

3arabawy Hossam عمو حسام
The protests have spontaneous leaders in most of the occasions. We won't let this uprirsng to be hijacked by anybody.
15:16:40 Jan 30

3arabawy Hossam عمو حسام
Situation in Suez is catastrophic in terms of deaths and injuries. The police fought the people in the same way Israelis fight Palestinians
15:19:28 Jan 30

3arabawy Hossam عمو حسام
There is no love whatsoever the protesters hold towards the US govt and Obama. They r hypocrites.
15:21:36 Jan 30

3arabawy Hossam عمو حسام
The Popular Committees hold the seeds for what direct democracy could look like in the future. We need to focus on them instead of BARADIE!
15:22:31 Jan 30

3arabawy Hossam عمو حسام
Demonstrations continue in all Egyptian cities. People do not want Omar Suleiman. People want to see Mubarak on trial.
15:23:58 Jan 30

3arabawy Hossam عمو حسام
State Security Police Stations in Daqahliya, Kafr El-Sheikh, Rafah, Damanhour, and in many other places have been torched down by protesters
15:25:13 Jan 30

Graffiti: No to Mubarak the US client
Photograph by @3arabawy Hossam el-Hamalawy - www.arabawy.org

3arabawy Hossam عمو حسام
Pigs at Nasr City Police Stations 1 & 2 have barricaded themselves inside the stations, shooting live ammunition at proteters from inside.
15:26:27 Jan 30

3arabawy Hossam عمو حسام
Gotta leave now and head back to the protests. Down with Mubarak. Down with Obama the hypocrite. Long live the Egyptian revolution.
15:41:35 Jan 30

Sandmonkey Mahmoud Salem
word is army has permission to shoot live ammunition at protesters #jan25
15:46:47 Jan 30

Gsquare86 Gigi Ibrahim جيجي
There r now fighter jets in the air trying to scare the protesters to leave Tahrir sq but NOTHING will stop the REVOLUTION until MUBARAK OUT
16:00:31 Jan 30

TravellerW Mo-ha-med
16 hrs of curfew a day. Police completely disappeared from Cairo. Neighbourhood watches keeping order. We are not broken yet. #Jan25 #Egypt
16:01:43 Jan 30

Gsquare86 Gigi Ibrahim جيجي
I am living through the Egyptian Revolution and i am sooo happy an proud, I wish my mom was alive to see this day ...
16:10:37 Jan 30

beleidy Amr El Beleidy
Curfew has started 10 minutes ago, tons of people on the street, it's not only Egyptian parents who can't enforce curfews #Jan25 Egypt
16:12:26 Jan 30

Gsquare86 Gigi Ibrahim جيجي
Fear is over in EGYPT !!! Fear has left the people and now with Muabark
16:14:12 Jan 30

sharifkouddous Sharif Kouddous
sitting next to my uncle. He's been protesting alone on the streets for years. "this is a dream come true," he says #Egypt
16:23:33 Jan 30

Sandmonkey Mahmoud Salem
we just had an air show of military planes flying at low altitudes tryin 2 scare ppl #jan25
16:30:54 Jan 30

TravellerW Mo-ha-med
Everytime a plane flies over Tahrir, demonstrators point out and say "hey, is that Mubarak finally leaving?" #Egypt #Jan25 :-)
16:31:21 Jan 30

Sandmonkey Mahmoud Salem
crowd in tahrir keeps growing. We're not going anywhere #jan25
16:32:03 Jan 30

TravellerW Mo-ha-med
A friend called from #Iraq to check if we were okay in #Egypt.
There was a demo in Gaza yesterday to support us. Huh.
#Jan25
16:50:32 Jan 30

beleidy Amr El Beleidy
Hearing from multiple news sources that @ElBaradei is now
going to Tahrir Square to address protesters #Jan25 Egypt
18:04:12 Jan 30

sharifkouddous Sharif Kouddous
Baradei seen as non-corrupt, is respected. But he lived away
too long, didn't join earlier protests & this revolt was done w/o
his help
18:54:41 Jan 30

sharifkouddous Sharif Kouddous
Big part of crowd sitting down to hear/see Baradei speak
#Egypt
19:11:20 Jan 30

norashalaby Nora Shalaby
egyptian residents sweeping the streets and keeping order in
neighborhoods, mubarak's strategy not working! #jan25
19:13:56 Jan 30

monasosh monasosh
Just came back from tahrir, ppl r still there, we r talking
100000 + #Jan25
19:22:55 Jan 30

monasosh monasosh
Curfew is on so no transport atall, had to walk, share a cab wt
ppl then walk again.Every few steps ppl formed check points
#Jan25
19:23:56 Jan 30

monasosh monasosh
This is something everyone has to know, I have never felt
safer, well protected in my country as i did today. #Jan25
19:25:01 Jan 30

sharifkouddous Sharif Kouddous
People saying Baradei fainted or something and went home.
People standing up and leaving disappointed. #Egypt
19:27:07 Jan 30

monasosh monasosh
I don't know why did we have police in the 1st place.
We seem to be taking good care of each other,organizing
traffic,cleaning streets #Jan25
19:31:54 Jan 30

sharifkouddous Sharif Kouddous
Lots of rumors spreading thru square. Baradei definitely
spoke but unclear if he left and if so why. Trying to find out
#Egypt
19:43:22 Jan 30

TravellerW Mo-ha-med
Slogans went frm "the Ppl Demand the Fall of the Regime" to
"..of the President". Reshuffling th political deck won't fool us.
#Egypt #Jan25
20:54:19 Jan 30

monasosh monasosh
@marcducharme I run from tahrir to where we have internet,
tweet and upload pics and videos then run back :)
21:16:51 Jan 30

Sandmonkey Mahmoud Salem
with curfew, no restaurants, food or gas. Basic goods will
soon b in shortage #jan25
21:19:42 Jan 30

Sandmonkey Mahmoud Salem
curfew tomoro 3pm to 8 am. They're trying to lock ppl in
&drive them insane #jan25
21:26:20 Jan 30

ashrafkhalil ashraf khalil
#Jan25 I'm at a hotel room overlooking Tahrir square and the
crowd is loud and jubilant.
00:17:36 Jan 31

ashrafkhalil ashraf khalil
#Jan25 I watched TV for an hour this morning and got really scared. Then I went outside and it was borderline jubilant out there
00:20:03 Jan 31

ashrafkhalil ashraf khalil
#Jan25 Army tanks were blocking the entrance to Tahrir today, but only to check demonstrators IDs and check for weapons.
00:21:12 Jan 31

ashrafkhalil ashraf khalil
#Jan25 But happy vibe in Tahrir between crowds and military somewhat soured by bizarre aggressive fighter jet flyover.
00:23:22 Jan 31

TravellerW Mo-ha-med
Still a few hundred people holding the fort in Tahrir. They were circling the square at rapid pace... It's a chilly night. #Jan25 #Egypt
00:40:39 Jan 31

TravellerW Mo-ha-med
I spoke to @Ghonim's brother and he is indeed missing since Friday. Lawyers have been informed and will start inquiring. Rabbena ye7meeh.
01:24:36 Jan 31

8

"THE ARMY AND THE PEOPLE ARE ONE HAND"

...as the Army promises not to fire on protesters

 RiverDryFilm Omar Robert Hamilton
Tahrir: volunteers collecting litter. People singing. Painting.
Like Glastonbury with tanks. And without Bono. #jan25 #egypt

IT WAS REPORTED THAT the army had defied orders from Hosni Mubarak to fire on protesters. Strong resistance from ordinary soldiers had filtered up the chain of command, and the top brass had their own interests to think of. The Egyptian Army, a huge institution whose elite had amassed vast economic assets since the military coup of 1952, received over a billion dollars of US aid each year. It was thought to be reluctant to put that funding at risk by using American weapons on unarmed civilians. Hosni Mubarak, an airforce general, may have been one of their own, but that did not mean he suited their purposes now. In fact the army had its own issues with the regime – it reportedly disliked the aged dictator's son, Gamal, who many expected to take over from his father.

An army statement to the protesters told them that "The presence of the army in the streets is for your sake and to ensure your safety and wellbeing. The armed forces will not resort to use of force against our great people." It called the protesters' demands "legitimate."

ashrafkhalil ashraf khalil
#Jan25 7 am and the 1st thing I hear is the word BATIL (illegitimate!) coming through balcony door from Tahrir.
07:22:54 Jan 31

ashrafkhalil ashraf khalil
#jan25 Israel lobbying hard to save Mubarak. How very touching... http://tinyurl.com/5sfhn5j
09:22:11 Jan 31

monasosh monasosh
Wael Ghonim from Alex, Marketing manager of Google Egypt & activist, no one can trace him since Friday #Jan25
11:48:26 Jan 31

3arabawy Hossam عمو حسام
Police is creeping back to some neighborhoods in Cairo. It started v late last night. Officers I've seen so far r only from traffic police.
12:11:21 Jan 31

3arabawy Hossam عمو حسام
The protests in Tahrir yesterday were very strong. We were more than 100,000 in the square.
12:17:17 Jan 31

3arabawy Hossam عمو حسام
I walked back from Tahrir to Nasr City yesterday, saw popular committees. Many shabab with swords said they'll kill cops if they show up.
12:19:09 Jan 31

3arabawy Hossam عمو حسام
More protests r scheduled today in Alexandria, Mahalla and other cities. Thousands of protesters r now in Tahrir already. Numbers will swell
12:22:13 Jan 31

3arabawy Hossam عمو حسام
The army is protecting police stations that haven't been burnt down. Traffic police officers stay close to army personnel for protection.
12:32:11 Jan 31

3arabawy Hossam عمو حسام
Internet is still blocked on ISPs: TEDATA and Link. I'm using a sattelite connection via a journalist friend now. It's VERY SLOW however.
12:47:43 Jan 31

Gsquare86 Gigi Ibrahim حبيبتي
I am back for a few..The police is fuckin back on the streets and WE WILL NOT STOP!!! It is me or them at this point!!
12:47:48 Jan 31

Gsquare86 Gigi Ibrahim حبيبتي
The people are calling for a million-plus people march tomorrow, which will be marking a week since #Jan25
12:53:30 Jan 31

Gsquare86 Gigi Ibrahim حبيبتي
The people have waited 30 years for this, no way will back out now!! The people or Mubarak in this country!!!
13:21:41 Jan 31

3arabawy Hossam عمو حسام
To our Arab brothers and sisters, if you want to support our intifada, overthrow your dictators. We need a regional intifada.
13:29:14 Jan 31

monasosh monasosh
I feel I haven't said it recently, FUCK YOU MOBARAK #Jan25
13:39:51 Jan 31

3arabawy Hossam عمو حسام
I spoke with a trade unionist in Suez now. The protests continue. Popular committees r running security. Police has vanished.
13:53:59 Jan 31

monasosh monasosh
Important: if u read reports of shotguns heard don't take it too seriously,we don't even budge when we hear them. We r really safe! #JAn25
13:57:05 Jan 31

monasosh monasosh
If i get 1 more call from my Bourjois friends abt hardship of
protecting their neighborhood & how they live in fear I will kick
them #Jan25
14:31:32 Jan 31

monasosh monasosh
You want Mobarak out? stop whining, get off ur asses and join
us in the streets #Jan25
14:33:18 Jan 31

beleidy Amr El Beleidy
Tahrir Square is a massive festival, morale is high, numbers
are huge, the lawyers were there when I was, ppl and army
are super nice #Jan25
14:38:34 Jan 31

beleidy Amr El Beleidy
I'm hearing of the new cabinet now, I should say cabinet there
is nothing new about it!! #Jan25 Egypt
14:51:50 Jan 31

monasosh monasosh
This is getting better, the awesome @3arabawy has joined us
here at the " Tweeting center of the revolution" #Jan25
15:02:11 Jan 31

3arabawy Hossam عمرو حسام
Army helicopter is now circulating. Forget it Hosni. That will
not terrorize us. You r finished!
16:49:29 Jan 31

Gsquare86 Gigi Ibrahim جيجي
The plan is to get Mubarak out, there is no organization, the
people are the ones driving the revolution !!
16:51:30 Jan 31

Gsquare86 Gigi Ibrahim جيجي
The revolution is being twitterized even with the internet being
shut by the government #Egypt
16:56:27 Jan 31

monasosh monasosh
Ok focus, shower, clean clothes atlast, then WORK then Hit the road !
16:56:50 Jan 31

beleidy Amr El Beleidy
Just moved my car to block the end of the street, porter telling me story about catching policemen last night in the street
17:04:33 Jan 31

beleidy Amr El Beleidy
He said the same men who used to hit us, insult us and our mothers were like mice in a trap...
17:05:36 Jan 31

TravellerW Mo-ha-med
Festive ambiance at Tahrir square. Few politicians, lots of people. Plenty of humorous banners - everyone more relaxed today. #Jan25 #Egypt
19:43:37 Jan 31

Photograph by @TravellerW Mohamed Al-Rahhal - www.travellerwithin.com

TravellerW Mo-ha-med
#Army major (ra2ed) I just spoke to: "even if they order us to shoot at demonstrator, I will not". #Egypt #Jan25
20:06:48 Jan 31

ashrafkhalil ashraf khalil
#Jan25 Army setting up dozens of fresh concrete barriers around Tahrir. Army guys have been great so far, but That feels like ominous sign.
20:43:55 Jan 31

ashrafkhalil ashraf khalil
#jan25 If Army tries to restrict protester movement tmw it's going to go very bad very quickly. Crowds tmw should be massive and motivated
20:45:08 Jan 31

RiverDryFilm Omar Robert Hamilton
Tahrir: volunteers collecting litter. People singing. Painting. Like Glastonbury with tanks. And without Bono. #jan25 #egypt
20:54:22 Jan 31

monasosh monasosh
statement from the army official spokesman stated that they r aware of the legitimate demands of the ppl & will not use violence them Jan25
21:09:15 Jan 31

ashrafkhalil ashraf khalil
#Jan25 Army announcement that it acknowledges peoples grievances and won't turn weapons on citizens is a HUGE relief.
22:27:49 Jan 31

ashrafkhalil ashraf khalil
#Jan25 the Black and white Mubarak-or-the-Brotherhood choice is dead. It died this week
22:37:04 Jan 31

monasosh monasosh
#Jan25 I think this different wave of protesting in Egypt started wt #KhaledSaid I truly believe that his death changed something in us all
22:40:40 Jan 31

TravellerW Mo-ha-med
General mood on the street is "he's started to give
concessions, so he's afraid - so we should press ahead until
he's gone" #jan25 #Egypt
22:43:12 Jan 31

Sandmonkey Mahmoud Salem
tuesday is the big day, pray for us guys we need your support
#jan25
03:29:24 Feb 1

9

TUESDAY, FEBRUARY 1
THE MILLION MAN MARCH

...as Tahrir Square stages a "festival of freedom" and Mubarak begins his counteroffensive

Sandmonkey Mahmoud Salem
today is the big day :) going out soon. heard that girls r getting their mothers to join. People getting friends. Everyone is going. #jan25

WITH THE TIDE OF PUBLIC OPINION *favoring the protesters, new Vice President Suleiman indicated he would start talks with opposition parties over constitutional reforms. But the initiative was not with the old opposition. Power now lay in the street, and protesters hoped to show just that with a million man march.*

Despite most internet services still being blocked, the turnout was huge. Tahrir thronged as the veterans of January 25 were joined by people who had never before been to a protest. They were the poor; the middle class; the rich; men; women, covered and uncovered; Muslims; Christians; whole families – all chanting and enjoying the humorous banners.

At the end of the day Hosni Mubarak took to the airwaves for his second speech of the uprising. In a concession, he pledged that he would not run for a further term as president, but insisted that he would stay on until scheduled elections in September.

The reaction from Tahrir was anger. The protesters had already defeated Mubarak's security forces and saw no reason to negotiate.

But Mubarak's strategy had a second dimension. Following his speech, pro-Mubarak supporters were mobilized. The counteroffensive was underway.

Sandmonkey Mahmoud Salem
news that Suleiman's been appointed by gov 2 negotiate w/
opposition leaders the demands of protests &constitutional
amendments.. #Jan25
09:02:39 Feb 1

Sandmonkey Mahmoud Salem
(cont.) these opposition leaders hav nothing 2 do w/protesters
#Jan25
09:04:05 Feb 1

Sandmonkey Mahmoud Salem
same opposition leaders who never managed 2 create a
sizable followin or gain 1 victory or get a rally that's 1% of
what we have now #Jan25
09:05:19 Feb 1

Sandmonkey Mahmoud Salem
today is the big day :) going out soon. heard that girls r getting
their mothers to join. People getting friends. Everyone is
going. #jan25
09:32:31 Feb 1

Sandmonkey Mahmoud Salem
I hope we do get our million man march today #jan25
09:32:48 Feb 1

ashrafkhalil ashraf khalil
Jan 25: Tweeting via my lovely wife abroad: last surviving
ISP finally shut down last night.
10:47:48 Feb 1

ashrafkhalil ashraf khalil
#Jan25: mass numbers expected today - everywhere in
Cairo, starting in Tahrir. Call for the people from the provinces
to flood the capital.
10:53:44 Feb 1

ashrafkhalil ashraf khalil
#Jan25: Mubarak ordered trains to shut down yesterday -
obvious attempt to limit access to Cairo
10:55:05 Feb 1

ashrafkhalil ashraf khalil
#Jan25: Fears that pro-Mubarak rally/thug-squad will try to spark violence. Protesters completely aware and expecting this.
10:57:55 Feb 1

Sandmonkey Mahmoud Salem
made it into tahrir. They shut down major entrances &making it very difficult to get in but thousands &thousands of ppl here. #Jan25
11:55:44 Feb 1

Sandmonkey Mahmoud Salem
We laughed today when we heard that Jordanian king sacked government preemtively. We're with you people of #Jordan #Jan25
19:58:23 Feb 1

#Jan25
Photograph by @3arabawy Hossam el-Hamalawy - www.arabawy.org

HOSNI MUBARAK APPEARS ON STATE TV

Sandmonkey Mahmoud Salem
i've never seen mubarak so nervous #jan25 #egypt
23:20:53 Feb 1

Sandmonkey Mahmoud Salem
he's trying to leave w/his dignity intact by finishing his term
but ppl wont accept this #jan25
23:22:06 Feb 1

Sandmonkey Mahmoud Salem
dilemma now: seems this is as far as mubarak is willing to go
&as far military will let him suffer #jan25
23:40:55 Feb 1

Sandmonkey Mahmoud Salem
some ppl say we shud let hm finish term, bt counter argument
is one more day of his failed leadership is 1day too much
#jan25
23:43:33 Feb 1

ashrafkhalil ashraf khalil
#Jan25 Mubarak's speech immediately rejected
00:20:12 Feb 2

ashrafkhalil ashraf khalil
#Jan25 They watched on a screen they had set up in Tahrir,
started chanting again 30 secs after
00:20:37 Feb 2

ashrafkhalilv ashraf khalil
#Jan25 with each new Mubarak half-concession, the crowd
gets more motivated, and more pissed off.
00:21:08 Feb 2

norashalaby Nora Shalaby
Mubarak thugs in alexandria and tahrir to scare people off the
streets #jan25
00:53:54 Feb 2

Photograph by @3arabawy Hossam el-Hamalawy - www.arabawy.org

 ashrafkhalil ashraf khalil
Seems like Mubarak seeking to entrench and lengthen the standoff and undermine public support for protestors.#Jan25
04:29:38 Feb 2

 ashrafkhalil ashraf khalil
His latest offer making some traction with many Egyptians. Some may be content to have him finish his term. #Jan25
04:30:23 Feb 2

 ashrafkhalil ashraf khalil
Raucous pro-Mubarak rally happening right now around the corner from Tahrir. Looks like about seven hundred people. #Jan25
05:38:21 Feb 2

 ashrafkhalil ashraf khalil
Pro Mubarak guys are on a stretch of the corniche where many Western TV stations have offices.#Jan25
05:39:10 Feb 2

 ashrafkhalil ashraf khalil
Only reason for pro Mubarak protestors at this hour is to get in background of U.S. primetime broadcasts.Somebody is being clever. #Jan25
05:42:38 Feb 2

10

BLOODY WEDNESDAY

...on which pro-Mubarak thugs attack the demonstrators in Tahrir Square with extreme violence

monasosh monasosh
This is a damn war zone, and the world is watching us!
#Jan25

AS EGYPTIANS WOKE *there was a new mood in the air. Hosni Mubarak's promise to step down in September appeared to have swayed segments of the population. The line that Mubarak should be allowed to leave "with dignity" was gaining traction, and many wanted life to get back to normal.*

Capitalizing on this loss of momentum, the regime encouraged and organized pro-Mubarak counterdemonstrations in the morning. But a more sinister plan soon became clear. The security forces were remobilized in plain clothes and were joined by paid thugs, directed to violently attack the demonstrators in Tahrir Square.

The scenes were horrific. A cavalry charge of thugs on horses and camels opened the hostilities, the riders whipping the crowd as they galloped through. Intense rock throwing between the two sides followed, as blood spilled in the streets. And the violence only intensified, with Molotov cocktails and later gunfire causing deaths and terrible wounds.

For hour after hour the fighting continued, relayed live on news channels across the world (although not on Egyptian state TV). The army simply stayed in their tanks, refusing to act. It looked certain that the protesters would be driven out – the attacks were relentless. But, remarkably, as darkness fell the protesters began to push the pro-Mubarak forces back. Advancing behind shields of corrugated iron and bits of car, like a ramshackle Roman legion breaking a siege, the youth, or "shabab," secured the streets, while in the rear makeshift medical centers cared for the wounded.

By dawn Tahrir Square was firmly under the control of the protesters. They would never lose it.

History is shaped by powerful economic and cultural forces, but sometimes it comes down to whether a few thousand people can hang on to a square overnight.

TravellerW Mo-ha-med
And a lovely revolution to you too, sir. Live from Cairo - we are back and excited like we've never been before! #Egypt #jan25
11:42:21 Feb 2

tarekshalaby Tarek Shalaby
Internet's back in #Egypt. I've been camping out in Tahrir for 4 days n will remain until #Mubarak leaves. #jan25
12:03:06 Feb 2

TravellerW Mo-ha-med
Eavesdropping on opposition meeting at Ghad party HQ. Serious arguing. Seems that Wafd is considering breaking ranks & talking to gov #Egypt
12:05:33 Feb 2

3arabawy Hossam عمو حسام
Here r the latest updates: The govt is countermobilizing against us now. There r several pro-Mubarak protests taking place in Cairo now.
12:20:04 Feb 2

norashalaby Nora Shalaby
Down w Mubarak graffiti that was all over city now being changed by pro-Mubarak thugs #Jan25
12:23:36 Feb 2

Sandmonkey Mahmoud Salem
The mood in Egypt today is different. Too many people still beholden to the mentality of slaves. This is so frustrating. #jan25
12:48:45 Feb 2

3arabawy Hossam حسام عمرو
We r at very critical stage. The counterrevolution is out in full steam. You will collect our dead bodies from garbage bins if we don't win.
12:49:48 Feb 2

Sandmonkey Mahmoud Salem
A lot of people talking on the street, saying that this is good enough, & we shouldn't forget what Mubarak did for us. The Irony baffles me.
12:50:15 Feb 2

beleidy Amr El Beleidy
The country seems to be splitting apart, fissures in my own family have already started
12:52:18 Feb 2

Sandmonkey Mahmoud Salem
We have foought for you, for accountability and change, and now that we are a hair away from victory, u betray us. #jan25
12:57:55 Feb 2

Gsquare86 Gigi Ibrahim جيجي
Testing the internet is working ? #Egypt
13:22:28 Feb 2

Gsquare86 Gigi Ibrahim جيجي
Omg I am finally tweeting from Tahrir square!!! I can't believe it finally #Jan25
13:27:10 Feb 2

Gsquare86 Gigi Ibrahim جيجي
Pro-Mubarak march now coming into Tahrir in 'a big number' and it will get ugly http://yfrog.com/h3zsgekj
13:39:10 Feb 2

Sandmonkey Mahmoud Salem
1000 pro Mubarak demonstration is heading towards Tahrir.
The military is withdrawing. This will get ugly quick #jan25
13:40:24 Feb 2

TravellerW Mo-ha-med
INCREDIBLE standoff between pro-change and pro-Mubarak
demos at Tahrir NOW #Egypt #jan25 http://twitpic.com/3vqkcp
13:40:49 Feb 2

gharbeia Amr Gharbeia
Now that's a really big pro-Mubarak protest almost reaching
Tahrir from Galaa Street #Egypt. Worrying.
13:44:53 Feb 2

TravellerW Mo-ha-med
Real panic in tahrir. Square overun by Mubarak drmonstrstion
#Egypt #jan25
13:46:50 Feb 2

TravellerW Mo-ha-med
I've seen spontaneous demos. The pro demo isn't one.
#Egypt #jan25
13:53:35 Feb 2

TravellerW Mo-ha-med
Pro-change demo has regrouped and is pushing back the
pro-Mub demo back to abdelmoneim Riyad sq #Egypt #jan25
13:57:47 Feb 2

TravellerW Mo-ha-med
Fuck reporting. I'm going in. #Egypt #jan25
14:07:46 Feb 2

TravellerW Mo-ha-med
Pro change chanting "SELMEYA" (PEACEFUL) #Egypt
#jan25
14:10:51 Feb 2

TravellerW Mo-ha-med
Pro change pulling each other away when possible violent
clash. Commitment to non-violence is remarkable. #Egypt
#jan25
14:12:07 Feb 2

Photograph by @sarahcarr Sarah Carr - www.inanities.org

3arabawy Hossam عمرو حسام
Clashes going on in Tahrir Square NOW. Mubarak has
mobilized thugs to attack protesters. #Jan25
14:25:14 Feb 2

TravellerW Mo-ha-med
Another pro Mubarak demo came storming from talaat harb
st- throwing stones. Stones def flying only in 1 direction: twrds
us. #Egypt #jan25
14:26:48 Feb 2

TravellerW Mo-ha-med
Where the FUCK IS THE ARMY IN ALL THAT? #Egypt #jan25
14:34:18 Feb 2

norashalaby Nora Shalaby
Is this mubaraks answer to us?? Sending thugs to throw stones at us! #Jan25
14:40:06 Feb 2

norashalaby Nora Shalaby
He couldn't beat us with his state security so he sends baltagiya to terrorize us. Down w the dictator #Jan25
14:41:17 Feb 2

TravellerW Mo-ha-med
People are chanting "Where is the army?" and "The people want the president to be prosecuted" #Egypt #jan25
14:44:32 Feb 2

monasosh monasosh
I am trying to upload what I have as fast as possible to run back to Tahrir #Jan25
14:49:21 Feb 2

3arabawy Hossam عمو حسام
Plainclothes thugs (police) are on horses now, trying to storm Tahrir Square, with whips! #Jan25
15:01:23 Feb 2

TravellerW Mo-ha-med
Army soldier:"we only stop ppl from entering w/ weapons" me: "they have bricks, man". Soldier waves and looks away. #Egypt #jan25
15:03:09 Feb 2

Sandmonkey Mahmoud Salem
Camels and Horses used by Pro Mubarak protesters to attack Anti-Mubarak protesters. This is becoming literally a circus. #jan25
15:04:27 Feb 2

Gsquare86 Gigi Ibrahim جيجي
I wanna puke..Mubarak wants blood of millions on the streets now!
15:31:54 Feb 2

Sandmonkey Mahmoud Salem
The aim of this is to evacuate the Tahrir square & justify never having protests there Friday, where 1 is scheduled, or ever again. #jan25
15:35:51 Feb 2

Sandmonkey Mahmoud Salem
Authoritarian Regimes, watch Mubarak and learn from the master. His regime doesn't fuck around. #jan25
15:37:04 Feb 2

beleidy Amr El Beleidy
This is turning into prehistoric war
15:49:04 Feb 2

tarekshalaby Tarek Shalaby
I can't believe Mubarak is willing to have his people kill each other just to keep his corrupt regime. #jan25
15:59:36 Feb 2

Gsquare86 Gigi Ibrahim جيجي
They r coming in with horses and thugs, we need more revolution people in Tahrir square now!
16:10:08 Feb 2

Gsquare86 Gigi Ibrahim جيجي
Everyone in Cairo who wants Mubarak out and stands for justice come to Tahrir NOW!
16:15:28 Feb 2

beleidy Amr El Beleidy
They're coming from all directions now, we're being surrounded
16:21:14 Feb 2

beleidy Amr El Beleidy
I came to a peaceful protest, this is not one!
16:30:50 Feb 2

norashalaby Nora Shalaby
Demonstrators r building barricades at all the entry points into tahrir #Jan25
16:42:21 Feb 2

Photograph by @sarahcarr Sarah Carr - www.inanities.org

ashrafkhalil ashraf khalil
#jan25 I saw at least a dozen guys coming back badly
bloodied from front line. Incredibly violent scene and the
soldiers are just watching
16:43:07 Feb 2

beleidy Amr El Beleidy
The hope of the whole region is now in one public square!
16:43:45 Feb 2

beleidy Amr El Beleidy
I have never even witnessed a street fight before, this is
overwhelming for me!
16:46:59 Feb 2

ashrafkhalil ashraf khalil
#jan25 Problem is that Tahrir has at least 9 streets leading
into it. Pro-Mubarak protesters probing the edges for soft
spots
16:49:35 Feb 2

ashrafkhalil ashraf khalil
#jan25 From what I saw, protesters were holding off charges
from multiple directions. But they're spread very thin to cover
all entranceways
16:50:16 Feb 2

ashrafkhalil ashraf khalil
#jan25 Crowd is very very angry. Saw a guy allegedly unmasked as a security agent and the crowd almost killed him.
16:52:00 Feb 2

ashrafkhalil ashraf khalil
#jan25 Other protesters basically saved the alleged security agent and pleaded with their colleagues for calm. Turned him over to soldiers
16:52:53 Feb 2

monasosh monasosh
Many are injured on the Egyptian Museum side #Jan25 They need help
16:53:25 Feb 2

Gsquare86 Gigi Ibrahim جيجي
Battle zone by kasr el nile bridge ..rock throwing back and forth, many injured http://yfrog.com/h4kr3rvj
17:13:49 Feb 2

monasosh monasosh
Cut wounds, fractures, rupture eyes. Weapons used glass, coke bottles, knives, swords #Jan25
17:20:10 Feb 2

Ssirgany Sarah El Sirgany
Just to recap. over a million demanding change in Egypt's streets yesterday. No violence. Today, pro-mubarak ppl are out and all out war.
17:25:03 Feb 2

beleidy Amr El Beleidy
Another injured friend!
17:26:32 Feb 2

beleidy Amr El Beleidy
He Was trying to protect a little girl! Captured people are with weapons, knives, some police!
17:28:03 Feb 2

Gsquare86 Gigi Ibrahim حبيبي
Every thug we confiscate we find that his I.D. says 'police'
those r the only pro-Mubarak supporters in #Egypt
17:32:36 Feb 2

norashalaby Nora Shalaby
Protesters putting on cardboard helmets for protection against
rocks #Jan25
17:48:04 Feb 2

Photograph by @sarahcarr Sarah Carr - www.inanities.org

Gsquare86 Gigi Ibrahim حبيبي
The Tahrir liberators are way less in numbers than the
Mubarak thugs if this continues more ppl will die! MUBARAK
OUT NOW!
17:56:49 Feb 2

monasosh monasosh
Every1 who is in other areas should take 2 the streets and
protest! Ppl in tahrir cannot hold their ground agnst all thugs
of egypt! #Jan25
18:01:16 Feb 2

TravellerW Mo-ha-med
Pro-Mubarak thugs are police. This is POLICE MASSACRING
CIVILIANS, make no mistake. #Egypt #Jan25
18:01:53 Feb 2

tarekshalaby Tarek Shalaby
I'm fine but we're under serious attack and there's no way out. I'm staying to the very end. Hasta la victoria, siempre. (@ FraCicardi)
18:10:08 Feb 2

TravellerW Mo-ha-med
Super violent stone throwing at Qasr El Nil bridge. Automatic rifle being shot. #Egypt #Jan25
18:10:37 Feb 2

tarekshalaby Tarek Shalaby
This is OUR revolution, and no one can take it away from us. #jan25
18:11:50 Feb 2

Gsquare86 Gigi Ibrahim جيجي
Liberation square is being protected by the brave youth..we are beating the thugs even with our few numbers..We WILL GET HIM OUT!
18:24:42 Feb 2

TravellerW Mo-ha-med
Man in the megaphone is shouting names to reunite families that were separated in the mayhem #Egypt #Jan25 #Freedom
18:26:47 Feb 2

TravellerW Mo-ha-med
Army tank by Qasr El Nil bridge ON FIRE!! #Egypt #Jan25
18:38:14 Feb 2

Sandmonkey Mahmoud Salem
Mubarak would rather burn down Egypt than leave it seems. #jan25
18:42:26 Feb 2

ManarMohsen Manar Mohsen
Pro-Mubarak thugs are breaking the bricks of sidewalks on their way to Tahrir Square. Overheard them say how they "will break their bones."
18:48:36 Feb 2

TravellerW Mo-ha-med
I am seeing - not reporting, seeing - Mubarak ppl throwing
,molotov cocktails on demonstrators, and on shops. #Egypt
#jan25
18:58:48 Feb 2

mosaaberizing Mosa'ab Elshamy
Got hit by some stones in the leg and one in the head but
nothing serious. Most important thing is we're flooding Tahrir
once again. #Jan25
18:59:06 Feb 2

Gsquare86 Gigi Ibrahim جيجي
The battles are horrific, pressure Mubarak to step down NOW
to save Egypt
19:05:16 Feb 2

Gsquare86 Gigi Ibrahim جيجي
The situation is escalating by the minute, we WILL NEVER
GIVE UP! Down with Mubarak and his thugs!
19:11:13 Feb 2

3arabawy Hossam عمو حسام
The shabab totally evicted Mubarak's thugs from Talaat
Harb. Tahrir is still under control of the shabab. Long live the
revolution. #Jan25
19:15:23 Feb 2

MohammedY Mohammed Yahia
100's injured in Tahrir in Egypt & at least 2 dead. Pro-Mubarak
thugs r throwing molotoves and huge slabs from rooftops on
protesters #Jan25
19:28:24 Feb 2

Gsquare86 Gigi Ibrahim جيجي
Gun fire from talaat harb st. We are in a battle field
19:28:39 Feb 2

MohammedY Mohammed Yahia
WE STILL HOLD TAHRIR SQUARE #Jan25 #Egypt
19:29:33 Feb 2

NevineZaki Nevine
anyone with Blood type O , please go and donate to your
nearest hospital. They are in massive shortages of type O
#jan25 #egypt
19:31:11 Feb 2

Gsquare86 Gigi Ibrahim جيجي
Haytham Mohamadain saying Talaat Harb sq has been
secured by the liberators ..we r winning :) http://yfrog.com/
h0grbytj
19:33:46 Feb 2

monasosh monasosh
I am where they keep the injured, ppl helped us pass through
the flying glass and shots. The shots were in the air to scare
thugs #Jan25
19:35:27 Feb 2

Gsquare86 Gigi Ibrahim جيجي
I WILL NOT LEAVE TAHRIR TONIGHT so stop telling me to
do so! We need more people in TAHRIR NOW!! Get here for
our freedom!!! #Egypt
19:39:22 Feb 2

mosaaberizing Mosa'ab Elshamy
The thugs have no cause or belief to fight for. They're only
doing this for money and are scared. We're psychologically
winning. #Jan25
19:55:51 Feb 2

monasosh monasosh
My friend's young brother is hurt in his head close to his eye,
he got 5 stiches. He is 17 yrs old for god's sake #Jan25
19:57:23 Feb 2

monasosh monasosh
2 from Mobarak's thugs were wounded, they were carried by
our ppl to be treated here, their hand were tied #Jan25
20:01:49 Feb 2

MohammedY Mohammed Yahia
When protesters capture thugs who r KILLING them, they
protect them from being beaten all the way till they hand them
to the military #Jan25
20:03:22 Feb 2

mosaaberizing Mosa'ab Elshamy
Incredible role played by women in Tahrir: delivering water,
carrying & aiding the injured, even breaking large stones.
#Jan25
20:03:47 Feb 2

MohammedY Mohammed Yahia
Outside Tahrir Square, nearly everyone is blaming us
protesters 4 the bloodshed! Ppl call me to tell me we should
"back down" #Jan25 #Egypt
20:05:12 Feb 2

Gsquare86 Gigi Ibrahim جيجى
The confiscated thugs have confessed that they were paid 50
LE to come and protest pro-Mubarak by central forces
20:12:06 Feb 2

Gsquare86 Gigi Ibrahim جيجى
At Kasr El Nile bridge, we have taken complete control Gaza
style with just rocks against gun fire http://yfrog.com/h0yzsgj
20:23:59 Feb 2

MohammedY Mohammed Yahia
Ppl still call me to tell me protesters should step down. I'm
sorry, the blood of the martyrs who died for freedom is too
precious #Jan25
20:49:24 Feb 2

norashalaby Nora Shalaby
All streets seem to be barricaded well and calm except for
museum area. Ambulances allowed to pick up injured #Jan25
20:54:27 Feb 2

Gsquare86 Gigi Ibrahim جيجى
Mubarak supporters are throwing fire from tops of buildings
on Tahrir protesters ..there are loud shooting sounds coming
frm that direction
22:10:38 Feb 2

mosaaberizing Mosa'ab Elshamy
Very tense near musuem now. We're still blocking them but
fatigue & injuries slowly catching up with us. More people
needed. #Tahrir #Jan25
22:31:39 Feb 2

mosaaberizing Mosa'ab Elshamy
We're now using burnt CSF trucks for protection & blockade
and pushing them away. Great advantage! #Jan25 #Tahrir
22:35:31 Feb 2

Gsquare86 Gigi Ibrahim حبيبح
I wish I could give u the noise the revolution is making in
Tahrir, it screams >> Get OUT!! #Mubarak http://yfrog.com/
h71vbchj
22:45:52 Feb 2

monasosh monasosh
This is a damn war zone, and the world is watching us!
#Jan25
22:57:36 Feb 2

Sandmonkey Mahmoud Salem
Anti-Mubarak protesters are descending on downton in the
thousands. They are not giving up Tahrir. #JAN25
23:00:59 Feb 2

mosaaberizing Mosa'ab Elshamy
Despite the blood and the pain, spirits here are sky-high.
People singing the anthem & waving flags while throwing
stones. #Jan25 #Tahrir
23:03:37 Feb 2

mosaaberizing Mosa'ab Elshamy
YES! We've pushed them away from the musuem! They're
running like rats. #Tahrir #Jan25
23:17:09 Feb 2

mosaaberizing Mosa'ab Elshamy
Abd EL Meneim Reyad square is ours now. Long live
revolution. #Jan25 #Tahrir
23:20:09 Feb 2

ManarMohsen Manar Mohsen
People on Kasr El Nil Bridge are battling with those below, on
both sides they are throwing rocks and petrol bombs. #Egypt
#Jan25
23:28:32 Feb 2

mosaaberizing Mosa'ab Elshamy
The musuem battle was the toughest today. Took over 8 hours. Huge win. #Tahrir #Jan25
23:29:11 Feb 2

mosaaberizing Mosa'ab Elshamy
Got hit. Elbow bleeding.
23:35:52 Feb 2

ManarMohsen Manar Mohsen
Seeing people move easily throu check points of tanks w/ soldiers as they carry bags of what appears to be rocks on Kasr ElNil Bridge #Jan25
23:51:42 Feb 2

Gsquare86 Gigi Ibrahim جيجي
Liberation square has won the battle in front of museum http://yfrog.com/h8ug5tzj
00:03:11 Feb 3

mosaaberizing Mosa'ab Elshamy
A crying woman just came to me, pleading, "Please, son, don't let them in. You know what they'll do to me & my kids." #Jan25 #Tahrir
00:09:42 Feb 3

ManarMohsen Manar Mohsen
To those who believed that 'Mubarak will finally bring change' after yesterday's speech, hopefully today made you think twice. #Egypt #Jan25
00:23:54 Feb 3

beleidy Amr El Beleidy
I did not take part in the violence, which is a real moral dilemma for me right now, for it's the people who did who saved me
00:53:00 Feb 3

mosaaberizing Mosa'ab Elshamy
Tonight could be the defining night of our revolution. If we hold on, millions will join us tomorrow and there'll be no stopping us.
01:00:00 Feb 3

mosaaberizing Mosa'ab Elshamy
Currently tweeting from behind a metal barrier directly
separating us from Mubafuck thugs. Saved my head from
hundreds of stones. #Jan25
02:16:26 Feb 3

beleidy Amr El Beleidy
The 3 injuries to my group of friends were 1 rock to the lip, 2
stitches, one rock to the head and moltov burns on the hand/
forearm
02:37:34 Feb 3

beleidy Amr El Beleidy
The sound of mass banging of rocks against metal is
something that will stay with me for some time
02:53:44 Feb 3

mosaaberizing Mosa'ab Elshamy
At least 80% of people here are bruised/bandaged. You'll pay
for this, Mubafuck. #Tahrir #Jan25
02:57:24 Feb 3

mosaaberizing Mosa'ab Elshamy
Mubarak thugs firing bullets at us now at Abd El Meneim
Reyad square. Dozens injured. #Tahrir #Jan25
03:35:47 Feb 3

mosaaberizing Mosa'ab Elshamy
General state: thousands of thugs bombarding us with
molotov & stones from October bridge. We're keeping our
high lines and defending well.
03:51:38 Feb 3

monasosh monasosh
Ppl r using the car ruins & rubbish around them 2 create
shields to advance to the frontline. I feel as if reporting on a
battlefield #Jan25
03:52:17 Feb 3

monasosh monasosh
Some1 among the thugs on bridge had a riffle, took his time &
aimed, 3 wounded, 1 dead, army to intervening #Jan25
04:06:34 Feb 3

mosaaberizing Mosa'ab Elshamy
THE BRIDGE IS OURS! #Tahrir #Jan25
04:14:58 Feb 3

mosaaberizing Mosa'ab Elshamy
My God! Our friends are waving to us from the bridge! #Tahrir
04:19:00 Feb 3

monasosh monasosh
The 3 wounded were in the ambulance infront of us, dead one
was from an eye witness account. The gun shots cld b heard
by any1 here #Jan25
04:27:12 Feb 3

mosaaberizing Mosa'ab Elshamy
The martyr at Abd El Meneim Reyad was carried and passed
in front of me about 15 minutes ago. #Tahrir
04:43:14 Feb 3

mosaaberizing Mosa'ab Elshamy
People are devastated for the martyrs. Praying for them and
chanting against Mubarak. Very emotional scenes. #Tahrir
04:50:35 Feb 3

mosaaberizing Mosa'ab Elshamy
We're very tired but everyone is staying up to see the
daylight. Still in disbelief over the day's events. #Tahrir
04:59:47 Feb 3

waelkhairy88 Wael Khairy
Oh God. The sound of gunfire! Machine guns echo can be
heard everywhere. God help us all.
05:01:00 Feb 3

monasosh monasosh
2 of my friends confirm another one is shot through the
head, dead. My friend called me crying #Jan25 this is awful,
something has 2 b done
05:29:33 Feb 3

waelkhairy88 Wael Khairy
Updates: 13 injured and 4 dead as a result of a few minutes of gunfire.
05:34:04 Feb 3

waelkhairy88 Wael Khairy
Gunfire came from above the 6th of October bridge..protestors went up there and arrested them
05:38:51 Feb 3

mosaaberizing Mosa'ab Elshamy
A final wave with few armed thugs carrying machine guns taking place now. Some more martyrs. #Tahrir
05:46:14 Feb 3

waelkhairy88 Wael Khairy
The tanks are moving. Two dead men are being dragged from bridge after being shot dead.
05:47:21 Feb 3

mosaaberizing Mosa'ab Elshamy
I'm on the bridge now. We're awaiting them. #Tahrir
05:53:12 Feb 3

mosaaberizing Mosa'ab Elshamy
We're fighting on the bridge now. They don't exceed 100. We need to hold on for 30 more minutes. #Tahrir
06:06:20 Feb 3

mosaaberizing Mosa'ab Elshamy
Sunrise in Cairo. Blood spilled in Tahrir more noticed now. All over the place. #Jan25
06:39:10 Feb 3

11

FORTRESS TAHRIR

...the Square emerges from the battles stronger than before

alaa Alaa Abd El Fattah
there are thousands of heros in the streets of Egypt today, I'm
humbled to be among them #Jan25

AT DAWN THE FULL HORROR OF THE NIGHT *before was laid bare. More than ten had died; over a thousand were injured. The area of the fiercest battle near the Egyptian Museum looked like a bomb had hit it, with charred sheets of metal and a carpet of rubble.*

In the morning the army made an attempt to dampen the violence, moving to clear pro-Mubarak thugs from a flyover near the museum. But clashes continued throughout the day on a smaller scale. Inside the barricades Tahrir was replenished by fresh supplies of food and medicine, and the number of protesters increased as the pro-Mubarak mobs diminished.

The Mubarak counteroffensive had new targets. All over Cairo journalists were subjected to attacks. Correspondents for major news organizations, including CNN and Al Jazeera, were beaten and detained. The Hisham Mubarak Law Centre (no relation to the president), a key human rights institution, was raided and several were arrested, as was a group that had been meeting Mohamed ElBaradei. State-run media whipped up fears of the shadowy outside interests it claimed were behind the uprising. Mobs began hunting foreigners.

While denying any responsibility for the attacks on journalists or the assaults on Tahrir, the regime offered further political concessions in an attempt to isolate the protesters. Vice President Suleiman confirmed that Hosni Mubarak's unpopular son would not run for president and revealed that he had offered to talk to the Muslim Brotherhood, although they, along with ElBaradei, refused to talk to him until Mubarak resigned.

alaa Alaa Abd El Fattah
there are thousands of heros in the streets of Egypt today, I'm
humbled to be among them #Jan25
08:48:03 Feb 3

Gsquare86 Gigi Ibrahim جيجي
Anyone capable of walking and has a heart and may be some
blood, COME TO TAHRIR and protect YOUR brothers and
sisters! #Egypt
09:43:05 Feb 3

TravellerW Mo-ha-med
Walking through the tahrir battlefield. Number of injuries
staggering. Morale impressively high. It really is "La
Resistance"! #Egypt #jan25
09:43:17 Feb 3

monasosh monasosh
Charging my mobile,on a balacony overlooking Tahrir square,
absorbing the horror of last night & the bravery of our ppl
#Jan25
09:54:52 Feb 3

gharbeia Amr Gharbeia
The resistance I witnessed in Tahrir last night is humbling.
We all owe it to the bravery of last night's Museum Battle in
#Egypt
09:59:29 Feb 3

Treating the injured
Photograph by @3arabawy Hossam el-Hamalawy - www.arabawy.org

ashrafkhalil ashraf khalil
#Jan25 entering tahrir. Vigorous multistage patdown to enter.
Also checking I'd cards for evidence you work for interior
ministry
10:00:24 Feb 3

beleidy Amr El Beleidy
Three days ago the sound of gunfire and helicopters used
to put me on edge, today got used to them I don't even blink
#Jan25 Egypt
10:51:22 Feb 3

monasosh monasosh
The ppl here are amazing! They are still chanting peaceful
peaceful even after we lost some of us during the worst nights
ever #Jan25
11:20:00 Feb 3

beleidy Amr El Beleidy
The PM says they're talking to opposition, the opposition says
they're not talking. Who exactly are they talking to? #Jan25
Egypt
12:24:54 Feb 3

3arabawy Hossam عمو حسام
in Tahrir. If u wand to come, go via bab el louq or qasr el nil
bridge.
12:28:31 Feb 3

MohammedY Mohammed Yahia
Just got 2 tweets at the exact same time, one saying go to
Tahrir through Qasr El Nil bridge and other saying don't.
Please confirm! #Jan25
12:30:34 Feb 3

monasosh monasosh
Friend was trying to deliver medical supplies, they smashed
his car and he had to turn & run away #Jan25
12:34:11 Feb 3

ashrafkhalil ashraf khalil
#jan25 just made narrow escape from mob in dokki. A soldier
saved us
12:37:12 Feb 3

Gsquare86 Gigi Ibrahim جيجي
Koshary on wheels to feed the revolution :) ..Koshary is a full nutritious
vegetarian Egyptian meal http://yfrog.com/h09atiej

norashalaby Nora Shalaby
Just got stopped by thugs at medan galal. Wouldn't let me
pass. Almost assaulted me.#Jan25
12:40:20 Feb 3

3arabawy Hossam عمو حسام
barricades r up around the square, watchmen bang on iron
bars whenever thugs approach to alert protesters.
12:42:35 Feb 3

ashrafkhalil ashraf khalil
#jan25 soldier who saved us from crowd now keeping us in
walled courtyard for safety. Found crew of other journo also
hiding here
12:51:39 Feb 3

NevineZaki Nevine
A pic I took yesterday of Christians protecting Muslims during their
prayers #jan25 http://yfrog.com/h02gvclj

Gsquare86 Gigi Ibrahim جيجي
A pro-Mubarak thug attacked this man with a knife at the museum
battle field last night #Tahrir http://yfrog.com/h8tt2gj

monasosh monasosh
Hisham mubarak law center, the leading law center in egypt is
currently surrounded by thugs and army police #Jan25
13:31:41 Feb 3

Ssirgany Sarah El Sirgany
State TV should be prosecuted for panic and mob mentality
they are spreading. People turning against each other in Cairo
streets
13:32:55 Feb 3

RamyYaacoub Ramy Yaacoub
I just called @SandMonkey 's phone and a man answered
and he asked me who I am, I said where is monkey, he said
your cunt friend is arrested
13:44:52 Feb 3

TravellerW Mo-ha-med
50 yr old little lady: I stopped coming to demo after Mub's
speech - but yesterday's attacks were so horrible I am now
back" #Egypt #jan25
14:07:39 Feb 3

3arabawy Hossam عمرو حسام
there must b 100,000 protesters at least today, sretching out
across Tahrir and side streets.
14;19:33 Feb 3

monasosh monasosh
Last I heard @sandmonkey was his car was smashed while he was trying to deliver supplies to us, he ran away,now he might be arrested #Jan25
14:19:57 Feb 3

Gsquare86 Gigi Ibrahim جيجي
No one should come to Tahrir alone, come in groups, some are being being arrested!
14:27:48 Feb 3

Gsquare86 Gigi Ibrahim جيجي
This is a man who wants a humane dignified life. State-media is calling him a 'terrorist' http://yfrog.com/gypvcrpj

3arabawy Hossam حسام عمر
the shabab r doing fantastic job @ the barricades. security is well run on all exits. Bless them.
15:02:43 Feb 3

monasosh monasosh
They arrested my father & all brave human rights lawers, called them spies for hamas & iran so the ppl would turn against them #Jan25
15:11:57 Feb 3

monasosh monasosh
The regime is trying all dirty tricks, arresting honest ppl,
sexually harassing girls,setting off their thugs & we r becomin
stronger #Jan25
16:01:10 Feb 3

3arabawy Hossam عمرو حسام
this is people's power. This democracy from below. This is the
most beautiful thing i have ever seen in my life.
16:20:23 Feb 3

alaa Alaa Abd El Fattah
Amazing atmosphere at tahrir, the joy is back in the square.
Massive crowd singing dancing we cannot be defeated
#Jan25
16:54:29 Feb 3

ashrafkhalil ashraf khalil
#Jan25 Confirmed 1st person that Shahira Amin deputy
director of state-run Nile TV has resigned in protest over
biased coverage
16:59:09 Feb 3

monasosh monasosh
Clashes back 1 of us wounded carried to medics, & they
arrested one of them,chanting peaceful to prevent protesters
from harming the thug
17:01:59 Feb 3

Injured
Photograph by @3arabawy Hossam el-Hamalawy - www.arabawy.org

Photograph by @TravellerW Mohamed Al-Rahhal - www.travellerwithin.com

Sandmonkey Mahmoud Salem
I am ok. I got out. I was ambushed & beaten by the police, my phone confiscated , my car ripped apar& supplies taken #jan25
17:51:15 Feb 3

mosaaberizing Mosa'ab Elshamy
Clashes still going on in October bridge area. Dozens of thugs captured and our resistance remains high. #Tahrir
18:11:10 Feb 3

Sandmonkey Mahmoud Salem
Please don't respond to my phone or BBM. This isn't me. My phone was confiscated by a thug of an officer who insults those who call.
18:23:38 Feb 3

MohammedY Mohammed Yahia
Egypt VP Suliman: There are only a few young people in Tahrir now and these are the ones who follow certain agendas #Jan25 Obv he needs a TV
19:03:12 Feb 3

MohammedY Mohammed Yahia
Egyptian VP: The young ppl should know that ALL their
demands were met. #Jan25 Ok so how can we get it thru to
them we want Mubarak out!?
19:06:33 Feb 3

MohammedY Mohammed Yahia
Egyptian VP: TV channels charged ppl with anger. #jan25 No
stupid, ppl are charged when their countrymen and women
are brutally killed
19:10:41 Feb 3

MohammedY Mohammed Yahia
On to Tahrir Square news. Today was a great day. Spirits are
high. Ppl playing music and singing patriotic songs. Spirits are
high! #Jan25
19:19:10 Feb 3

MohammedY Mohammed Yahia
Oh and the Egyptian Museum is safe! I was really worried
when ppl talked about molotovs burning in the front garden of
the museum #Jan25
19:21:59 Feb 3

mosaaberizing Mosa'ab Elshamy
Heartbreaking. A young man in tears, devastated for just
knowing about the loss of his brother today morning. #Tahrir
19:37:15 Feb 3

Gsquare86 Gigi Ibrahim جيجي
Head to Tahrir as early as you can tomorrow, we want to give
them a day of rage like they have given us days of violence &
injustices
20:44:54 Feb 3

MohammedY Mohammed Yahia
Why is the regime TOTALLY silent towards #journalists
attacked today? Why are they allowed to get away with shit
like that? #Jan25 #Egypt
21:08:03 Feb 3

Gsquare86 Gigi Ibrahim جيجيج
I am so exhausted in every way possible, but I can't shut my
eyes in peace knowing that Mubarak is still in power
21:08:04 Feb 3

mosaaberizing Mosa'ab Elshamy
A small group of thugs on October bridge now. Not attacking
us. Just chanting pro-Mubafuck slogans and insulting
Baradei. #Tahrir
21:24:00 Feb 3

mosaaberizing Mosa'ab Elshamy
It's basically a face-off with both groups waiting for other one
to start the stone-throwing. We'll only hit back if they start.
#Tahrir
21:27:26 Feb 3

mosaaberizing Mosa'ab Elshamy
The thugs are actually chanting "we love you, daddy!" -
بنحبك يا بابا . lol #Tahrir #Mubafuck
21:37:42 Feb 3

mosaaberizing Mosa'ab Elshamy
A real heartfelt moment when we chanted "We're all
Egyptians", they applauded in return and chanted with us.
#Tahrir
21:43:15 Feb 3

Gsquare86 Gigi Ibrahim جيجيج
hmmm activists disappearing and journalists are being beaten
up, keep an eye on me, i might be next
21:45:01 Feb 3

3arabawy Hossam عمو حسام
Since I'm getting asked this a lot from non-Arabic speakers:
Shabab means youth. :) #Jan25
21:50:47 Feb 3

mosaaberizing Mosa'ab Elshamy
Another sleepless night. Patroling Talaat Harb entrance now.
#Tahrir
22:12:45 Feb 3

3arabawy Hossam عمو حسام
So in sectarian country like Egypt, how many churches have been attacked since the uprising started? ZERO! Revolution changes people. #Jan25
22:36:06 Feb 3

sharifkouddous Sharif Kouddous
Hundreds of people are sleeping next to each other in the grassy area in the middle of the square. Packed together close. #Egypt
22:46:56 Feb 3

mosaaberizing Mosa'ab Elshamy
Few ambulance cars left Tahrir now carrying today's injured and killed ones. #Tahrir
23:03:21 Feb 3

sharifkouddous Sharif Kouddous
People have routed power from the street lights and are charging their cell phones in Tahrir #Egypt
23:04:00 Feb 3

RamyRaoof Ramy Raoof
Tomorrow 4 Feb i will Join People of #Egypt a demonstration against Mubarak & the Regime in Tahrir Square. I Invite All to Join. #Jan25
23:27:40 Feb 3

mosaaberizing Mosa'ab Elshamy
Our so called intellectuals should come and observe the lovely political discussion groups going on between normal Egyptians in Tahrir.
23:49:37 Feb 3

mosaaberizing Mosa'ab Elshamy
Remember, this is a nation that only waved the flag during football games and was labelled by its past PM "not yet ready for democracy".
23:55:38 Feb 3

mosaaberizing Mosa'ab Elshamy
There are 7 routes leading to Tahrir square. We set up barricades and numerous lines of defence on everyone. Hundreds patroling. #Tahrir
00:22:53 Feb 4

Fences to guard and entrance to Tahrir Square
Photograph by @ramyraoof Ramy Raoof - www.ebfhr.blogspot.com

mosaaberizing Mosa'ab Elshamy
The toughest attacks were yesterday and still failed.
Everything else today fades in comparison. We're doing
great, really. #Tahrir
00:45:58 Feb 4

monasosh monasosh
I know u ppl will think I am exagerating but Tahrir square is
the safest place in cairo right now! And it is cozy :) #Jan25
00:49:13 Feb 4

sharifkouddous Sharif Kouddous
People are being rounded up. Reports of 20+ ppl detained
from rights groups like El Baradei's, Hisham Mubarak's,
Amnesty, HRW... #Egypt
00:58:31 Feb 4

monasosh monasosh
Hope my dad is warm wherever he is. Sweet dreams #Jan25
02:44:40 Feb 4

mosaaberizing Mosa'ab Elshamy
As far as I know, no plans whatsoever tomorrow on marching
to presidential palace/embassies/ministeries/State TV. Just
pack Tahrir more.
02:47:19 Feb 4

 mosaaberizing Mosa'ab Elshamy
Our power lies in occupying Tahrir for the longest duration
with more people. Very obvious how it's driving the regime
crazy.
02:51:52 Feb 4

12

THE DAY OF DEPARTURE

...on which protesters try through sheer numbers to force Mubarak out

omareldeeb Omar El-Deeb
I was wrong, I thought today was going to be a bloodbath! It's
beautiful. #jan25

*AFTER THE HORROR of the previous days came relief and celebration. The
numbers that assembled after Friday prayers, on the traditional day off in
the Arab world, were huge – a fitting vindication for those who had risked
their lives to hold the Square.*

*Public opinion, which had wavered after Mubarak had promised to go
by September, had been outraged by the violence brought to central Cairo
by the regime, and impressed at the strong and dignified response of the
protesters.*

*But as evening fell on the Day of Departure there was one problem –
Mubarak had not departed. Democratic debate intensified among protesters.
Tahrir Square, which now had stages and PA systems, had become a huge
forum of political discussion on how to nonviolently escalate the uprising.*

*Many wanted to march on the Presidential Palace. It was thought the
move would force the army to finally decide between the regime and the
People, but it was risky. Backed into a corner, the army might side with
the president, and protesters were loath to leave the Square undefended.
There was also the practical problem of the Presidential Palace being several
kilometers away, in the district of Heliopolis.*

*Another initiative was to outline a political way forward beyond Mubarak.
One suggestion called for the removal of the entire regime, including Vice
President Suleiman, followed by a transitional government to oversee the*

country while a committee would write a new constitution.

Others around the world were looking for a solution, too. There were media reports that behind the scenes the US was pressuring the Egyptian Army and elite for a quick handover of power from Mubarak to Suleiman, ditching Mubarak to save the regime.

 wael Wael Khalil
from Tahrir sq. we're waking up and getting ready, chants are going already, Leave Leave #egypt #jan25
07:03:24 Feb 4

 monasosh monasosh
Good morning ppl, I can feel the energy! #Jan25
07:12:52 Feb 4

 mosaaberizing Mosa'ab Elshamy
Good morning, fellow freedom fighters.
08:15:51 Feb 4

 Sandmonkey Mahmoud Salem
The regime wanted to get rid of the foreign media, so they spread tales of terrorist foriegn spies, to justify attacking journalists. #jan25
08:24:50 Feb 4

 mosaaberizing Mosa'ab Elshamy
Breakfast now being distributed and shared. Families living in Tahrir are doing an amazing job in their solidarity. #Jan25
08:32:35 Feb 4

ashrafkhalil ashraf khalil
#jan25 #egypt Protesters in tahrir already chanting loud.
They're calling today the "Day of Departure" for Mubarak
08:36:14 Feb 4

mosaaberizing Mosa'ab Elshamy
Mohammed El Beltagy, prominent figure in Muslim
Brotherhood, talking to protesters now. Will highlight most
important issues. #Tahrir #MB
08:36:26 Feb 4

mosaaberizing Mosa'ab Elshamy
The Muslim Brotherhood will NOT run for presidential
elections, have no interest in being part of a post-revolution
government. #MB #Tahrir
08:45:45 Feb 4

ashrafkhalil ashraf khalil
I'll be doing a phone interview on state-owned Nile TV in
15 minutes. This should be fun! I'm amazed they called me
#jan25 #egypt
09:02:03 Feb 4

ashrafkhalil ashraf khalil
And yes, this is the same channel whose deputy Director
Shahira Amin resigned yesterday in protest over biased
coverage #jan25 #egypt
09:06:17 Feb 4

ashrafkhalil ashraf khalil
It's been a really terrible two days, but messing with Nile TV
people live on the air was the most fun I've had in a while.
#Jan25 #egypt
09:40:27 Feb 4

MohammedY Mohammed Yahia
My bestfriend's friend was shot & killed on Wednesday.
Thousands went out to his funeral in Makram Ebeid St.
honoring martyrs' blood #Jan25
10:14:04 Feb 4

mosaaberizing Mosa'ab Elshamy
We're positive and hopeful about today but we know revolutions take weeks, if not months, and we're ready for that. #Tahrir
10:35:44 Feb 4

TravellerW Mo-ha-med
Just got home. Beaten up, detained by the army, and spent part of the night in a kind soul's home in Zeinhom. Life's good! #Egypt #Jan25
11:42:40 Feb 4

monasosh monasosh
U need to be here, listen to the chants and clapping to feel how intensely powerful this is #Jan25
11:45:25 Feb 4

TravellerW Mo-ha-med
THANK YOU to all those who worried, called, tweeted about me. Nothing better than friends, real or virtual, one can count on. :) #Egypt
11:45:42 Feb 4

TravellerW Mo-ha-med
When detained I saw several journos - two Swiss and two US, at least - also detailed. Were taken to jail. In a tank. #Egypt #Jan25
11:47:05 Feb 4

TravellerW Mo-ha-med
2 army officers were 3 metres away when I was being beaten up by the pro-Mub mob. Did abso-fucking-lutely nothing. #Egypt #Jan25
11:50:34 Feb 4

beleidy Amr El Beleidy
A lot of women and old people here, people meet people they know, it's a social scene #jan25 egypt
12:10:04 Feb 4

mosaaberizing Mosa'ab Elshamy
New comers applauded by us but foreigners are met with extra cheers. #Tahrir
12:24:48 Feb 4

Gsquare86 Gigi Ibrahim حبيبي
I have goose bumps ..liberation square http://yfrog.com/
h2oselbj
12:30:55 Feb 4

Gsquare86 Gigi Ibrahim حبيبي
Amazing scene here..I am living through a historical moment
http://yfrog.com/h8we4czj
12:31:34 Feb 4

Sandmonkey Mahmoud Salem
The scene of Tahrir right now is incredible. Millions of people
praying. Reverence. Very powerful. It looks like Mecca in haj.
#jan25
12:38:23 Feb 4

Gsquare86 Gigi Ibrahim حبيبي
Many people are crying now as they are praying for the dead
.. :(#Tahrir
12:39:45 Feb 4

mosaaberizing Mosa'ab Elshamy
Guard of honor formed for new comers. Absolutely
heartwarming. #Tahrir
12:42:21 Feb 4

pakinamamer Pakinam and Voice
People please understand that mass prayers are a form
of protest, not necessarily a display of religiously, but unity
#Jan25 #Tahrir #Friday
12:43:25 Feb 4

beleidy Amr El Beleidy
The numbers are crazy, feels way more than Tuesday, I feel safe. Tahrir square #jan25 egypt
12:54:54 Feb 4

monasosh monasosh
Egyptian are chanting, this is the youth's revolution, this is the people's revolution #Jan25
12:57:03 Feb 4

3arabawy Hossam عمو حسام
there must b at least half a million protesters in the square and we haven't even started! #jan25
13:00:43 Feb 4

Sandmonkey Mahmoud Salem
What's in Tahrir right now is the best kind of escalation required from the protesters. They responded to the regime magnificently. #jan25
13:04:29 Feb 4

MohammedY Mohammed Yahia
Thousands standing at #Tahrir square entrance cheering the ppl coming in. The energy is AMAZING! #jAN25
13:08:35 Feb 4

Sandmonkey Mahmoud Salem
Tahrir is bursting to its seams from people, and thousands more coming. They could end up filling the area until the 6 October bridge.#jan25
13:13:33 Feb 4

3arabawy Hossam عمو حسام
come to Tahrir if u r in cairo and watch history in the making. #jan25
13:14:33 Feb 4

MohammedY Mohammed Yahia
Ppl chanting "stay strong oh my country! Freedom is being born" #Jan25
13:15:41 Feb 4

pakinamamer Pakinam and Voice
Very touching picture! #Jan25 #army #Egypt (via @Elazul)
http://yfrog.com/h5pm0gxj

Zeinobia Zeinobia
Amr Moussa in Tahrir
13:38:16 Feb 4

mosaaberizing Mosa'ab Elshamy
Some others walking with Koshary (famous Egyptian dish)
defying the KFC propaganda proposed by government.
#Tahrir
13:43:35 Feb 4

ashrafkhalil ashraf khalil
There is a catapult assembled on Kasr El Nil St. A
CATAPULT! Picture coming once I figure out how to work
Twitpic #jan25#egypt
13:43:41 Feb 4

ashrafkhalil ashraf khalil
The egyptian revolution: Facebook, Twitter, mounted calvary
charges and catapults. Weirdest revolt ever...#Egypt#jan25
13:47:06 Feb 4

mosaaberizing Mosa'ab Elshamy
About the Koshari tweet, Pro-mubarak media said we're only staying at Tahrir because foreign powers are giving us KFC meals.
13:48:15 Feb 4

ashrafkhalil ashraf khalil
Here's that catapult from Tahrir Square #egypt #jan25 http:// twitpic.com/3wdbss
13:49:05 Feb 4

mosaaberizing Mosa'ab Elshamy
Worth noting that KFC branch at Tahrir was looted and broken by thugs, weeks ago.
13:49:36 Feb 4

MohammedY Mohammed Yahia
I have met dozens of friends i havent seen for many years today in #Tahrir Square. Everyone is here! #Jan25
13:50:28 Feb 4

ashrafkhalil ashraf khalil
Really conflicted about the catapult. I hope there's no violence and it's never used. But I kind of want to see it in action #jan25 #egypt
13:54:10 Feb 4

Sandmonkey Mahmoud Salem
The Qasr el neel bridge is overflowing with people marching in to Tahrir. In other news, there is a pro Mubarak demo in Mohandeseen of 3000
14:05:46 Feb 4

fakroona fakrouna ben fakroun
FREEDOM LOADING ▓
99% #Egypt #Jan25 #Tahrir #Cairo #mubarak #sidibouzid
#fridayofdeparture #yemen #syria #jordan
14:39:38 Feb 4

omareldeeb Omar El-Deeb
I was wrong, I thought today was going to be a bloodbath! It's
beautiful. #jan25
14:50:22 Feb 4

MohammedY Mohammed Yahia
everyone asks me what will we do if Mubarak doesn't leave.
The answer is simply. We'll be back tom and the days after till
he leaves #Jan25
15:18:54 Feb 4

Sandmonkey Mahmoud Salem
When this is over, Tahrir square will be the reason tourists will
come to Egypt from now on. #jan25
15:46:09 Feb 4

MohammedY Mohammed Yahia
I can't imagine better company than those around me. You
all humble me and I'm proud to be among you today and
everyday #Jan25
16:28:18 Feb 4

monasosh monasosh
u can't believe how amazing it is, crowd is HUGE, lines of ppl
extending over Kasr el nile bridge & beyond. Tahrir rocks wt
Egyptians #Jan25
16:45:30 Feb 4

monasosh monasosh
Stay tuned wt us in Tahrir square, watch us BRING
MUBARAK DOWN! #Jan25
16:50:08 Feb 4

Sandmonkey Mahmoud Salem
Some protesters are demanding a march on the presidential
palace and people are discussing it. #jan25
16:59:32 Feb 4

Singing for the Revolution
Photograph by @3arabawy Hossam el-Hamalawy - www.arabawy.org

monasosh monasosh
Unified chanting " we r not leaving,he is leaving " It is so powerful I feel like crying #Jan25 Baba should be here, I am sure he is safe :)
17:10:49 Feb 4

Sandmonkey Mahmoud Salem
It doesn't seem like they will march to the presidential palace. The mood is not ready. #jan25
17:23:16 Feb 4

mosaaberizing Mosa'ab Elshamy
Sunset over Tahrir has never looked more gorgeous.
17:48:55 Feb 4

MohammedY Mohammed Yahia
Sporadic reports of attacks on #Tahrir Square but none are serious threat. Power in numbers and we are a million! #Jan25
18:02:20 Feb 4

beleidy Amr El Beleidy
People ignore all media and go see for yourself, don't fall for the propaganda, break the fear barrier #jan25 egypt
18:12:02 Feb 4

Photograph by @sarahcarr Sarah Carr - www.inanities.org

 pakinamamer Pakinam and Voice
Love or hate them, Muslim Brothers have legitimate demand
& they suffered at the hands of the regime. They have every
right to be in #Tahrir
18:16:18 Feb 4

 TravellerW Mo-ha-med
Am with friends, old and new, including people whose name
i don't know. Friendship and solidarity work well together! \m/
#egypt #jan25
18:21:00 Feb 4

 beleidy Amr El Beleidy
I passed by gam'it el dowal St where pro-mubarak demos are,
the amount of rubbish from 200 ppl contrasts with the super-
clean tahrir square
18:21:59 Feb 4

 monasosh monasosh
Tahrir square is the safest area in cairo, just becoz it is the
one area totally free of any interference of Mubarak's regime
#Jan25
18:43:06 Feb 4

mohamedahmos Mohamed Ahmos
FREEDOM LOADING ▓▓▓▓▓▓▓▓▓▓▓▓▓▓▓▓ 99% [
Error : Please remove Mubarak and try again !] #Jan25
#Egypt #Mubarak #Tahrir
19:09:00 Feb 4

TravellerW Mo-ha-med
Rumour gov is spreading to simple people is that
demonstrators are paid $50 & 2 KFC meals/day! That's
criminal incitement! #egypt #jan25
19:38:36 Feb 4

monasosh monasosh
Alexandria is witnessing a massive demo in Sidi Gaber, it
started raining and ppl are still there :) #Jan25
19:43:49 Feb 4

Gsquare86 Gigi Ibrahim جيجي
Vindication is soo sweet..I am at an awe
19:56:32 Feb 4

mosaaberizing Mosa'ab Elshamy
Loads of people intending on sleeping in Tahrir tonight. Learnt
from the mistake of leaving on Tuesday which made thugs'
job easier.
20:18:53 Feb 4

monasosh monasosh
Hearing horror stories abt what the regime is doing in secret.
The army is involved #Jan25
20:45:02 Feb 4

monasosh monasosh
The army is not neutral. The army is playing a filthy role
#Jan25
21:18:59 Feb 4

monasosh monasosh
Let me clarify something: violation stories I heard are
probably not by all army, but by militiary police #Jan25
21:49:43 Feb 4

Protesters' demands written on the building
Photograph by @3arabawy Hossam el-Hamalawy - www.arabawy.org

MohammedY Mohammed Yahia
As you head out of #Tahrir Square, ppl shake hands with
you & reminding u to come today and telling u to "get the
message out" #Jan25
22:05:32 Feb 4

MohammedY Mohammed Yahia
No one can imagine the beautiful feeling one gets as
you enter #Tahrir Square. It's like coming home & being
surrounded by loved ones #Jan25
22:06:49 Feb 4

mosaaberizing Mosa'ab Elshamy
Concerts are being held here, contests take place, and tents
are set up. We could stay in #Tahrir forever, Mr. President.
22:16:09 Feb 4

MohammedY Mohammed Yahia
I'm not very happy with Obama's current stance which he just
expressed in a press statement he made now- not asking
Mubarak to resign #Jan25
22:32:29 Feb 4

JanoCharbel Jano Charbel
My camera is stolen, my body is bruised and my eye is still black & blue, but I've never felt better in my life. #Egypt #Revoluton
23:49:06 Feb 4

Sandmonkey Mahmoud Salem
It's an outrage that Wael @Ghonim is still missing. Our hearts are with you. #jan25
00:12:42 Feb 5

ashrafkhalil ashraf khalil
Jan25# 1:30 am and the crowds in tahrir are still large and LOUD. Amazing stamina on these guys... #egypt
01:32:24 Feb 5

NevineZaki Nevine
I used 2 never leave home without lip balm in my bag, now it's switched to ID, tear gas mask & trash bags in a satchel! #fun #Egypt #jan25
02:53:14 Feb 5

monasosh monasosh
I need to sleep badly, went to a friend to rest, so for tonight Tahrir square is Mona seif free :) Good night #Jan25
03:21:24 Feb 5

monasosh monasosh
I have to get this out b4 I sleep: We should have marched today #Jan25
03:56:19 Feb 5

13

SATURDAY, FEBRUARY 5
THE PEOPLE ARE IN CHARGE

...as protesters resist the army and assert their control of Tahrir

mosaaberizing Mosa'ab Elshamy
We're sitting in front of their tanks after the army tried to remove the barricades we set up near the musuem. #Tahrir

THE TAHRIR ENCAMPMENT AWOKE to a tense scene as the army attempted to clear some of the barricades erected during Bloody Wednesday. The protesters were able to stop them, and also prevented any encroachment into the square by sitting down around the tanks and refusing to move. Whatever the intention of the army had been, by the afternoon protesters had seen it off.

Meanwhile there were further political developments. Vice President Suleiman began his much vaunted "national dialogue," meeting a group calling itself the "council of wise men." These putative opposition figures sought a compromise that would allow Mubarak to stay on in a symbolic role while handing power to Suleiman – a solution clearly unacceptable to Tahrir.

But the regime was starting to crumble from the inside. Many key officials in Mubarak's NDP party resigned their positions, including Mubarak himself, who stepped down from the presidency of the party – although not, of course, of the country.

The US position, which had gradually moved away from Mubarak, was undermined by President Obama's envoy, former ambassador Frank Wisner, who told the media he thought his old friend Mubarak should stay. The Obama administration distanced itself from his comments.

beleidy Amr El Beleidy
Good morning! What's in store for us today?
07:45:45 Feb 5

beleidy Amr El Beleidy
Got my answer quickly, a soar throat and a blocked nose!
07:52:57 Feb 5

mosaaberizing Mosa'ab Elshamy
Listening to some discussions going around, many fear how other Egyptians might slowly lose hope and turn against them. Could be a problem.
07:54:24 Feb 5

mosaaberizing Mosa'ab Elshamy
Some keep suggesting we march to presidential palace. We don't think its a good idea. Would jeopardize our safety by confrontation with army
08:03:16 Feb 5

mosaaberizing Mosa'ab Elshamy
The army is trying so hard to *look* neutral but we know they can't wait to find an excuse to take us down. Not giving them that. #Tahrir
08:06:32 Feb 5

3arabawy Hossam عمرو حسام
the army is moving in, trying to remove Barricades around Tahrir set up by protesters near Abdel Moneim Riyadh sq.
09:11:26 Feb 5

3arabawy Hossam عمرو حسام
10 mins earlier, Dr Beltagui of the Ikhwan asked protesters not to resist the army. He was booed
09:14:01 Feb 5

mosaaberizing Mosa'ab Elshamy
We're sitting in front of their tanks after the army tried to remove the barricades we set up near the musuem. #Tahrir
09:30:16 Feb 5

norashalaby Nora Shalaby
Ppl need to start heading towards #tahrir as it seems the
army has an agenda today #Jan25
09:34:43 Feb 5

mosaaberizing Mosa'ab Elshamy
Thousands of protesters surrounding them now, making it
clear the tanks will have to run them over before moving any
further. #Tahrir
09:38:28 Feb 5

monasosh monasosh
We have an info on where my dad is. He is fine. Hopefully will
be released today #Jan25
10:11:07 Feb 5

Sandmonkey Mahmoud Salem
The mood is tense!
10:40:10 Feb 5

Gsquare86 Gigi Ibrahim جيجي
The determination of the Tahrir protesters is stronger than
ever before,I know in my heart Mubarak WILL step dwn,the
revolution WILL succeed
11:11:00 Feb 5

mosaaberizing Mosa'ab Elshamy
"Twitter", "Facebook" and "Aljazeera" written in large letters on
walls of Tahrir. #Media #Tahrir
11:56:41 Feb 5

MSM, Social Media and the Egyptian Revolution
Photograph by @3arabawy Hossam el-Hamalawy - www.arabawy.org

3arabawy Hossam عمو حسام
the army is trying to ban people from entering Tahrir. The soldiers r trying to block Qasr el Nil bridge. #jan25
12:21:55 Feb 5

3arabawy Hossam عمو حسام
from day 1 i've been screaming: Do NOT trust the army. This is Mubarak's army not Egypt's army. #jan25
12:25:03 Feb 5

monasosh monasosh
My dad is out and safe #Jan25
12:59:53 Feb 5

mosaaberizing Mosa'ab Elshamy
There are hundreds of Army soldiers here. First day to see this huge presence from them. #Tahrir
13:04:45 Feb 5

mosaaberizing Mosa'ab Elshamy
The army wants to remove the barbed wires which were set up to stop thugs from coming in. We're trying to stop that. #Tahrir
13:26:40 Feb 5

battutta g RaDwaN
Army not letting cheese in! From asr il nil. Cheese! Only packaged food and bread,wtf? Whole line wants my cheese allowed in #jan25 #egypt
13:45:03 Feb 5

3arabawy Hossam عمو حسام
The army has allowed a group of 100 Mubarak's thugs into Qasr el-Nil bridge now. #Jan25
13:46:51 Feb 5

mosaaberizing Mosa'ab Elshamy
Army vehicle with microphone speaking now. Not saying anything positive. #Tahrir
13:49:38 Feb 5

norashalaby Nora Shalaby
A group of Mubarak thugs are chanting in front of the qasr el
nil check point obviously trying to intimidate us #Jan25
14:53:14 Feb 5

norashalaby Nora Shalaby
Also the army is only letting very few ppl in at a time which is
creating chaos bc thousands r trying to get in #Jan25
14:54:17 Feb 5

TravellerW Mo-ha-med
Army increasingly dislikes demonstrators, blaming them
for their deployment in Cairo's streets. Understandable, but
dangerous. #egypt #jan25
15:04:50 Feb 5

3arabawy Hossam عمو حسام
Tension between army & protesters is on the rise. I'm told an
officer shouted to protesters: Do u think u bought this square
with ur money?!
15:07:10 Feb 5

SawsanGad Sawsan Gad
@3arabawy Actually, yes, technically they did. They paid
taxes for the establishment of this square. Public space is
owned by everyone.
15:08:37 Feb 5

norashalaby Nora Shalaby
Raining here. Getting soaked #Jan25
15:36:26 Feb 5

battutta g RaDwaN
It was raining tear gas on jan28, regular rain is a relief, we not
going anywhere! #tahrir #jan25 samedoon! #egypt
16:07:01 Feb 5

3arabawy Hossam عتمو حسام
The sight of the crowds chanting in Tahrir now, waving flags,
under the rain, is gonna make me cry... #Jan25
16:54:35 Feb 5

Gsquare86 Gigi Ibrahim جيجي
I LOVE YOU EGYPT!!! #Tahrir #Revolution http://plixi.com/p/74824935

 waelkhairy88 Wael Khairy
Christians will pray in Tahrir tomorrow and we shall circle them
and protect them as they have protected us.
17:34:06 Feb 5

 tarekshalaby Tarek Shalaby
Personal analysis: govt changed strategy and is playing the
waiting game. We'd need to make a move by mid week to
keep momentum. #Jan25
17:38:09 Feb 5

 tarekshalaby Tarek Shalaby
Many are worried that the army will attack tonight. Maybe,
but I don't think they'd open fire. We're not going anywhere
#Jan25
17:39:46 Feb 5

 tarekshalaby Tarek Shalaby
The entire world and half of Egypt is behind us. The remaining
will follow when we bring them the revolution. Viva la
revolución! #Jan25
17:42:30 Feb 5

 Gsquare86 Gigi Ibrahim جيجي
It is starting to rain harder now..I feel it's a conspiracy ..it will
be rough night in Tahrir but people keep on coming :)
17:55:40 Feb 5

3arabawy Hossam عمو حسام
BBC: Hosni Mubarak resigns from the presidency of the NDP #Jan25
18:10:55 Feb 5

3arabawy Hossam عمو حسام
:D RT: @nmoawad: loool RT: @jamalghosn: Will Mubarak lead the opposition against the NDP? #jan25
18:24:33 Feb 5

Sarahcarr أبو كار
Resignation of NDP goons who have strangled Egypt 4 the past 30 yrs: brought to you by the heroes of Tahrir Sq #jan25
19:10:57 Feb 5

MennaAmr Menna Amr
That makes two of us. RT @Arabista Confused by the whole Mubarak NDP resignation fiasco.
19:35:12 Feb 5

Sambousak Peace and Justice
@Sandmonkey foreign press says Mubarak fortune estimated at 40 to 70 BILLION dollars!!! These must be returned to the people of Egypt!!!
20:11:31 Feb 5

mosaaberizing Mosa'ab Elshamy
More tents set up in the square as weather might be chilly/rainy tonight. Tahrir feels more like home everyday. #Tahrir
20:13:35 Feb 5

tarekshalaby Tarek Shalaby
From the 9th floor overlooking Tahrir sq. Amazing! #jan25
http://twitpic.com/3x3bxf

Sandmonkey Mahmoud Salem
http://1000memories.com/egypt For all of those who fell in our
fight for freedom: We remember and we are grateful! #jan25
21:09:38 Feb 5

monasosh monasosh
Rt now Tahrir sq, a meeting initially started wt 20 has turned
into 200 discussing how 2 counter trashing campaign of
national media #Jan25
21:37:18 Feb 5

TravellerW Mo-ha-med
Frank 'The Ass' Wisner says Mubarak should stay.
Disappointed that Obama is choosing short-term interests
over higher ideals. #Egypt @Jan25
22:07:58 Feb 5

Sandmonkey Mahmoud Salem
Dear Frank Wisner, Please keep your opinions to yourself.
Sincerely, the Egyptian people!
22:10:15 Feb 5

Sandmonkey Mahmoud Salem
Many people are asking me for the way forward, and so
far we seem to have 2 options: 1) remian as is & 2) the
wisemen's council #jan25
22:22:52 Feb 5

Sandmonkey Mahmoud Salem
The Wisemen's council is respectable, but am not sure what
leverage they got on either side.. #jan2
22:34:44 Feb 5

Sandmonkey Mahmoud Salem
But the status quo won't due. This lack of action and
organization will be used against us in every way possible .
#jan25
22:35:30 Feb 5

Sandmonkey Mahmoud Salem
Start registering the protesters, get their names, addresses &
districts. Start organizing them into committees. & they elect
leaders #jan25
22:38:22 Feb 5

pakinamamer Pakinam and Voice
Finally, I have known what the brethren and camaraderie of a revolution feels like. Trust me, it's precious. #Jan25 #Tahrir #Egypt
23:21:32 Feb 5

monasosh monasosh
Sms service is working in egypt again. Yaay let's plan a big demo #Jan25
00:32:38 Feb 6

tarekshalaby Tarek Shalaby
cold n rainy night in Tahrir sq. Has been very festive/ entertaining with songs n poetry. #jan25
04:10:58 Feb 6

tarekshalaby Tarek Shalaby
No sign of an open attempt to kick us out. MC trying to keep everyone up so we're ready to fight if needed. I think we're fine. #jan25
04:17:46 Feb 6

Reem_Ahmed Reem Ahmed Shalaby
A must see video !! Egyptian Revolution 2011 COMPLETE http://me.lt/3Tp8a #Egypt #Jan25 #Tahrir #IhaveAdream to see my lovely country better!
04:21:54 Feb 6

tarekshalaby Tarek Shalaby
At Tahrir sq. you can find pop corn, couscous, sweet potatoes, sandwiches, tea & drinks! Egyptians know how to revolt! #jan25
04:22:12 Feb 6

14

SUNDAY, FEBRUARY 6

A NEW THREAT

...as life outside Tahrir begins to get back to normal

 ManarMohsen Manar Mohsen
Banks open today, & people are going back to work. If u still support #Jan25, go to Tahrir to show that demands still need to be met. #Egypt

ON THE FIRST DAY OF A NEW WEEK the government attempted to get Egypt back to work. So far it had effectively shut down the economy; now for the first time banks reopened and people resumed their jobs. This was a change in strategy and a threat to the protesters. The regime's initial idea had been to create as much havoc as possible by withdrawing the police, blocking the internet, and closing the banks, expecting people to blame the uprising for the inconvenience. That having failed the government sought to isolate the protesters behind their barricades in the hope that the revolution would fizzle out.

On the political front Vice President Suleiman held inconclusive talks with more opposition forces, including representatives of the Muslim Brotherhood and the National Association for Change who had both previously refused to take part.

Inside the liberated zone an alternative normality had been created, complete with weddings and concerts. A bout of flu was making its way around the protesters, some of whom had been sleeping in tents or in the open for over a week.

TravellerW Mo-ha-med
Cairo traffic returning. Cabbie's comment: "a traffic mess -
traffic police must be back! We were doing fine without them!"
#Egypt #jan25
09:28:40 Feb 6

ManarMohsen Manar Mohsen
Banks open today, & people are going back to work. If u still
support #Jan25, go to Tahrir to show that demands still need
to be met. #Egypt
11:01:04 Feb 6

3arabawy Hossam عمو حسام
I'm reporting those who've Mubarak's pic as their Facebook
profile. It's for sure an "Inappropriate profile photo" and "Hate
symbol" #Jan25
11:27:47 Feb 6

norashalaby Nora Shalaby
Traffic back to normal. Long lines in front of banks #Jan25
12:59:16 Feb 6

mosaaberizing Mosa'ab Elshamy
If TV could transmit the genuine feeling of happiness around
Tahrir, I'm sure every other Egyptian would join us now.
13:19:02 Feb 6

monasosh monasosh
Concert at 3pm in Tahrir square, Salalem Band 7 Eskendrella.
Come & join us sing Mubarak away :) #Jan25
13:35:12 Feb 6

mosaaberizing Mosa'ab Elshamy
Saw a man wearing a refree kit and holding a large red card
with 'Mubarak, OUT' written on it. Football revolutionaries join
in. #Tahrir
13:44:23 Feb 6

monasosh monasosh
To those joining us in Tahrir, will be greatly appreciated if you
could get common cold medicines & vitamin C #Jan25
14:01:11 Feb 6

mosaaberizing Mosa'ab Elshamy
With many going back to their daily work, gotta say I'm surprised by the large turnout today. Very comforting. #Tahrir
14:18:06 Feb 6

norashalaby Nora Shalaby
Army trucks trying to advance again but protesters stand firm in museum area #jan25
14:36:23 Feb 6

norashalaby Nora Shalaby
Mubaraks coffin being carried around. On it is written: the funeral is in tel aviv #Jan25
15:42:20 Feb 6

ashrafkhalil ashraf khalil
Entering Tahrir area on foot felt like walking to a major outdoor rock concert or street festival. There were kids selling #egypt flags!
16:02:57 Feb 6

mosaaberizing Mosa'ab Elshamy
I know new steps have to be taken soon but the fact that we can still gather 100s of thousands for the 13th day is a huge feat. #Tahrir
16:18:36 Feb 6

tarekshalaby Tarek Shalaby
There's a couple that's about to have their katb el ketab (marriage ceremony) at Tahrir sq. in front of the revolutionary crowd! #jan25
16:22:55 Feb 6

ashrafkhalil ashraf khalil
@aymanm from Jazeera English has been arrested. He's been expecting it for days. Security forces have been asking for him by name. #egypt
17:48:36 Feb 6

ashrafkhalil ashraf khalil
Can someone please explain to me this government's obsession with Jazeera? And inability to grasp that harassing them will backfire? #egypt
17:50:40 Feb 6

ashrafkhalil ashraf khalil
Cynical/worrywart question of the day: will the #egypt
government try something while all of America is watching the
super bowl tonight
18:19:18 Feb 6

Sandmonkey Mahmoud Salem
I got many calls and emails from people living abroad who
want to help this uprising by sending donations. This is not a
good idea. #jan25
19:02:35 Feb 6

Sandmonkey Mahmoud Salem
The revolution has to be pure, and receiving outside funding
would be used to tarnish or attack it. There is a better idea.
#jan25
19:03:37 Feb 6

Sandmonkey Mahmoud Salem
Create a fund for the families of the victims of the government
crackdown on the #jan25 revolution instead, 2 help them
recover later #jan25
19:05:33 Feb 6

monasosh monasosh
We can hear gun shots, ppl r running towards the Egyptian
museum #Jan25
19:43:46 Feb 6

alaa Alaa Abd El Fattah
Proresters angry chanting against army, army shooting in the
air #Jan25
19:53:58 Feb 6

monasosh monasosh
The army were trying to block this entrance wt wire, ppl
prevented them,army shot in air to scare them and arrested 1
(maybe 5). #Jan25
19:56:14 Feb 6

monasosh monasosh
Eye witness: the boy was arrested by militiary army, and he
was severely beaten up, still not released #Jan25
20:12:09 Feb 6

norashalaby Nora Shalaby
I love how microbus drivers have begun congtegating outside
asr el nil every evening to take protesters home #Jan25
21:14:46 Feb 6

ashrafkhalil ashraf khalil
Omar suleiman statement today full of mixed messages.
Still talking "foreign intervention" but protesters "patriotic and
honorable" #Egypt
21:56:48 Feb 6

Sandmonkey Mahmoud Salem
The current situation in Egypt has unified many people
together, but has also driven other people incredibly apart.
#jan25
22:50:03 Feb 6

Sandmonkey Mahmoud Salem
The two camps are those who believe that Mubarak is lying &
buying time & should leave now, and the other believes he is
sincere. #jan25
22:50:55 Feb 6

Sandmonkey Mahmoud Salem
The "Mubarak is sincere" team is accusing us of not being
reasonable, and are totally adamant that he is leaving come
November. #jan25
22:51:54 Feb 6

Sandmonkey Mahmoud Salem
My fear is that if they have their way, he will stay till then,
produce some paid demonstrations for him to run again & he
will. #jan25
22:53:43 Feb 6

Sandmonkey Mahmoud Salem
Today, a christian mass was held in Tahrir, two people got
married, and a couple is spending their honeymoon there.
Awesome. #jan25
23:35:39 Feb 6

Sandmonkey Mahmoud Salem
The protesters are behaving with utter selflessness: people donating money, goods, medicine and time. Every1 looking out 4 each other #jan25
23:48:20 Feb 6

Fraggaman Fragg
@Sandmonkey If I had a $ for every goosebump this revolution has given me I would be richer than Mubarak!!
23:51:38 Feb 6

Gsquare86 Gigi Ibrahim جيجي
There is NO compromise, there is NO going back, there is NO backing down>>>Revolution Victory is the only option #Egypt
02:29:49 Feb 7

Gsquare86 Gigi Ibrahim جيجي
"Leave because I am cold" #Tahrir http://yfrog.com/gyqweiuj

15

THE WAEL GHONIM INTERVIEW

...when one man makes Egypt cry

 NevineZaki Nevine
everyone is crying, EVERYONE @Ghonim

THE DAY AFTER THE REVOLUTION STARTED, Wael Ghonim, a thirty-year-old marketing executive for Google, had been interviewed by prominent host Mona el-Shazly on Egyptian channel Dream TV. The following day he went missing.

While thousands of other activists had been detained during the protests, Ghonim's case became a symbol. Appeals were circulated online. Prominent figures including el-Shazly pressed for his release. Finally, after eleven days spent blindfolded in detention, he was freed and went directly to the TV studio to tell his story.

Wael Ghonim spoke from the heart. His television appearance was raw, unprepared, and tearful. It emerged that he had been one of the anonymous administrators of the We Are All Khaled Said Facebook page, which had circulated calls for the first demonstrations. He used his interview to explain to Egyptians, as he had explained to his state interrogators, that the protesters were not traitors or agents of foreign powers but young people simply demanding a better country. When el-Shazly showed pictures of some of those who had been killed in the protests, Ghonim broke down in tears and walked off set.

The tone of Wael Ghonim's interview, at that particular moment, won over the nation. He had gently exposed the brutality of the regime, and brought home with unsuppressed emotion the price that had been paid in blood. For those uncommitted Egyptians who were not yet revolutionaries, it was decisive. For the regime it was devastating.

alaa Alaa Abd El Fattah
it's amazing how strong yet fragile revolution is (or maybe that's norm for revolutions?) everyday is a test, everynight is pivotal #Jan25
07:30:36 Feb 7

beleidy Amr El Beleidy
Just got word my grandfather and aunt are planning to go to Tahrir today! The older generation are now in the game!
10:31:23 Feb 7

mosaaberizing Mosa'ab Elshamy
The mother of a martyr named Ramy was in Tahrir yesterday and spoke to the protesters. Very touching words. [1/3]
12:09:04 Feb 7

mosaaberizing Mosa'ab Elshamy
"Stay strong, my sons. Ramy died for you. He had no interested in politics & could barely buy a shirt for himself." [2/3] #Tahrir
12:10:04 Feb 7

mosaaberizing Mosa'ab Elshamy
"When Ramy heard of #Jan25 he said, 'I'm leaving, mum. I'm fed up. I can't live well or even marry. I'm going to get my rights.'" [3/3]
12:12:08 Feb 7

ManarMohsen Manar Mohsen
Lines stretching outside banks all over #Cairo. People crowding cafes and shops. But don't be fooled, they're all talking about #Jan25.
13:41:55 Feb 7

moftasa Mostafa Hussein
Tahrir square is the biggest brainstorming & think-tank in the middle east and possible the world now. #egypt #jan25
13:42:23 Feb 7

ashrafkhalil ashraf khalil
Video of unarmed protester gunned down, apparently from last week in Alexandria. Anybody have more info? #egypt
http://tinyurl.com/6yzqt9f
14:09:00 Feb 7

ashrafkhalil ashraf khalil
Todays arrests so far, Wael Abbas and Karim Amir. How can govt expect anyone to trust their promises when the KEEP ARRESTING people? #egypt
14:14:35 Feb 7

ashrafkhalil ashraf khalil
Important to note: outside festive Tahrir bubble, easy to find normal Egyptians fed up with revolution and disruption of normal life #egypt
14:18:24 Feb 7

3arabawy Hossam عمو حسام
people r sleeping around every single tank in the square to prevent the army from moving. #jan25
15:05:37 Feb 7

TravellerW Mo-ha-med
Surreal - people literally camping by the tanks!! #Egypt #Jan25
http://twitpic.com/3xgiy1

3arabawy Hossam عمو حسام
the tora cement workers have started a sit in over work conditions. #egyworkers #jan25
15:26:21 Feb 7

3arabawy Hossam عمو حسام
another sit in is going on now in Suez Trust Textile plant.
#egyworkers #jan25
15:27:28 Feb 7

3arabawy Hossam عمو حسام
we need industrial actions. We need the suez canal workers
and air traffic controllers to strike. #egyworkers #jan25
15:39:18 Feb 7

MohammedY Mohammed Yahia
Conflicting reports on whether Wael @Ghonim is out or not.
We need definite proof guys (preferably with pic) #Jan25
17:15:23 Feb 7

A child leading the chants
Photograph by @3arabawy Hossam el-Hamalawy - www.arabawy.org

Sandmonkey Mahmoud Salem
just came from tahrir. the crowds aren't dwindling. it's
becoming Tahrir Festival city. The energy is not abetting.
#jan25
17:55:07 Feb 7

Sandmonkey Mahmoud Salem
They now have giant murals of the pictures of those who died
posted everywhere. They made this possible. We will never
forget them. #jan25
17:57:17 Feb 7

Gsquare86 Gigi Ibrahim حبيب
For them, for us, for the future, the revolution must continue, Mubarak
must step down NOW! #Tahrir http://yfrog.com/h4isxswj

 monasosh monasosh
@ghonim release not confirmed. Plz wait till some1 send a
pic, or family member or friend confirms. Better report it late
than wrong #Jan25
18:11:21 Feb 7

 Ghonim Wael Ghonim
Freedom is a bless that deserves fighting for it. #Jan25
20:04:17 Feb 7

 Sandmonkey Mahmoud Salem
wael @ghonim is FREEEEEEEEEEEEEEEEEEEEEEE.
Kafarah :) #jan25
20:15:23 Feb 7

 Sandmonkey Mahmoud Salem
Now that @ghonim is out, let's get the rest out. Freedom to all
#jan25 prisoners. #jan25 #egypt
20:16:53 Feb 7

 Ghonim Wael Ghonim
Gave my 2 cents to Dr. Hosam Badrawy. who was reason
why I am out today. Asked him resign cause that's the only
way I'll respect him #Jan25
20:30:55 Feb 7

monasosh monasosh
Love this! Barber's corner in the square, wt a banner saying "
revolution's barber" #Jan25 http://yfrog.com/h38mutvj
21:56:33 Feb 7

monasosh monasosh
Ooh and hair cut is for free #Jan25
21:58:30 Feb 7

WAEL GHONIM APPEARS ON DREAM TV

Sandmonkey Mahmoud Salem
Wael looks incredibly humble. #dream2 #jan25
22:22:56 Feb 7

Sandmonkey Mahmoud Salem
"We are not traitors. We love Egypt." while crying..what's
going on? #jan25
22:25:33 Feb 7

Sandmonkey Mahmoud Salem
"The thing that killed me inside was that people found out that
i am the admin of Khaled Saeed. I didn't want people to know"
#jan25
22:26:19 Feb 7

Sandmonkey Mahmoud Salem
It must fuck him over that people have died because of what
he started on Facebook. @Ghonim It's not ur fault. #jan25
22:27:11 Feb 7

Sandmonkey Mahmoud Salem
" I was proud to be egyptian on the #jan25 . When there is a
lot of girls &no sexual harrassment, when people would stop
violent ones."
22:31:17 Feb 7

Sandmonkey Mahmoud Salem
"This is not the time to settle scores, this is not the time to cut
the cake, &this is not the time for enforcing ideologies" #jan25
@ghonim
22:36:02 Feb 7

Sandmonkey Mahmoud Salem
Correcting Mona.."My name is Wael, not Khaled. I would be
honored to be Khaled (Saeed)" @ghonim #jan25
22:42:32 Feb 7

Gsquare86 Gigi Ibrahim جيجي
I wish I was watching @Ghonim unfortunately I am in #Tahrir
22:44:48 Feb 7

TravellerW Mo-ha-med
Damn you, Mona Shazly. Now I'm crying too. #Egypt #Jan25

23:08:21 Feb 7

Sandmonkey Mahmoud Salem
DreamTV is showing pictures of those who died in #jan25 to
@Ghonim . He is crying. Mona Elshazly, wtf? #jan25
23:08:27 Feb 7

MennaAmr Menna Amr
Holy shit this is devastating.
23:08:27 Feb 7

MohammedY Mohammed Yahia
Wael @Ghonim cries when he sees the pictures of the people
who died #Jan25 #Egypt
23:08:44 Feb 7

Sandmonkey Mahmoud Salem
"I want to tell to everybody who lost a son, I am sorry. I swear this isn;t my fault. This is the fault of those who held to power"
@ghonim
23:09:51 Feb 7

NevineZaki Nevine
everyone is crying, EVERYONE @Ghonim
23:10:14 Feb 7

Sandmonkey Mahmoud Salem
@Ghonim left the studio right after saying that. This is so messed up. #jan25
23:10:29 Feb 7

NevineZaki Nevine
why did she have to show him the photos? WHY!
23:12:09 Feb 7

OmarElAdl Omar El Adl
Wael's brother and friends are all crying in the studio. Heartbreaking. #jan25
23:12:30 Feb 7

Sandmonkey Mahmoud Salem
Mubarak now has no choice but to go. #jan25
23:12:48 Feb 7

Sandmonkey Mahmoud Salem
MILLIONS WILL GO TO TAHRIR TOMORROW. MILLIONS!
#JAN25
23:14:06 Feb 7

ManarMohsen Manar Mohsen
Egyptians everywhere are crying with/for both Wael and Egypt. Show that you care, that the current state is not acceptable. Tahrir tomorrow!
23:21:22 Feb 7

TravellerW Mo-ha-med
The Wael @Ghonim interview will probably be the inspiration this revolution seemed to be losing. Bless you, friend. #Egypt #Jan25
23:21:37 Feb 7

ManarMohsen Manar Mohsen
Other guests on the show are fighting their tears. Wael @Ghonim's words are a turning point for all of us, there's no going back. #Jan25
23:25:34 Feb 7

tarekshalaby Tarek Shalaby
Living in Tahrir sq makes me live the glorious revolution, however I missed @Ghonim 's interview, so that sucks. Will YouTube tom. #jan25
23:52:04 Feb 7

Sandmonkey Mahmoud Salem
A revolution organized by facebook, spread by twitter and organized by a guy working for Google. #jan25 #ILOVEOURREVOLUTION
23:54:55 Feb 7

ashrafkhalil ashraf khalil
I don't personally know @ghonim but can't be more impressed with the guy. Tearful, sincere and raw interview on satellite TV tonight #egypt
00:01:17 Feb 8

NotHosniMubarak محمد حسني سيد مبارك
Suddenly starting to think that releasing Wael @Ghonim was probably not such a great idea. #Egypt #Jan25
00:04:59 Feb 8

MennaAmr Menna Amr
I've been terrified this revolution would fade but @Ghonim made that impossible. Thank you for being one hell of an inspiration for everyone
00:09:59 Feb 8

TheAlexandrian Youssef Chouhoud
Watching @Ghonim break down, I couldn't help but wonder if #Mubarak has ever shed a tear for a single life he's taken.
00:35:33 Feb 8

monasosh monasosh
12 days blindfolded completely cut off the world, nobody knows anything about him. This is awful #Jan25
00:36:54 Feb 8

ashrafkhalil ashraf khalil
Final thought for the night: anyone who's on the fence about #egypt protests, watch Wael @ghonim speak, then make up your mind #egypt
00:41:05 Feb 8

etharkamal Ethar El-Katatney
Tomorrow, millions will come to #tahrir. Tomorrow, things will happen and things will change. Tomorrow might just be the end #jan25
00:48:27 Feb 8

Sandmonkey Mahmoud Salem
The Wael Ghonim fb fanpage is getting 1000 fan each second. #jan25
01:01:21 Feb 8

Gsquare86 Gigi Ibrahim جيجي
Let's also not forget about all those who are NOT on twitter and facebook, who don't have bread to eat let lone computers or even TV
01:01:58 Feb 8

Gsquare86 Gigi Ibrahim جيجي
I doubt that people in Tahrir now where I am sleeping have revolted cuz of facebook but for why&how KhaledSaid was killed in the first place
01:24:32 Feb 8

monasosh monasosh
We want all our detainees out, we want Mubarak and his corrupted gang out. Let all Egypt be one glorious big Tahrir square #Jan25
01:26:39 Feb 8

Elazul Elazul
Mobarak lied on TV, and divided friends, families, loved ones. @Ghonim spoke the Truth, and he united everyone. #Jan25 Jan25
02:17:14 Feb 8

Sandmonkey Mahmoud Salem
Alarabiya says that Ahmed Zuweil and Mohamed ElBaradei refuse to negotiate now unless Mubarak leaves first. #jan25
02:19:29 Feb 8

Ghonim Wael Ghonim
When you don't see anything but a black scene for 12 days you keep praying that those outside still remember you. Thanks everyone #Jan25
03:32:02 Feb 8

16

TUESDAY, FEBRUARY 8
MOMENTUM REGAINED

...as massive demonstrations give the Revolution new impetus

 alaa Alaa Abd El Fattah
At last we are escalating #Jan25

EARLIER THE PREVIOUS DAY it had looked like the Revolution was losing pace. Life was getting back to normal. The foreign media was shipping out. The world's attention was waning. The regime's plan was working.

Tuesday, February 8, put an end to all that. The turnout in Cairo and in multiple cities and towns in Egypt was the biggest yet. Far from losing momentum, the Revolution was snowballing. And it was spreading into the workplace as strikes broke out around the country.

In Tahrir the numbers were so great that it was almost as if protesters were forced to branch out from the square just to make room for themselves. A group set off for the People's Assembly, a few blocks away, and occupied the street in front of it.

At the same time as protesters were advancing the regime was retrenching. Vice President Suleiman's national dialogue had come to nothing as he issued cryptic statements about the "dark bats of the night" and warned that the regime might be forced to launch a "coup against itself." "The culture of democracy is still far away," he said, while the rest of Egypt was out expressing its democratic will.

pakinamamer Pakinam and Voice
If you're going to #Tahrir, take Vitamin C tablets & if you already have a cold, wear a protective mask. Caught the flu, & it's crippling :(
08:02:46 Feb 8

mosaaberizing Mosa'ab Elshamy
Plans for another million man march today. Please 1) Come over. 2) Bring someone with you. 3) Get some supplies. #Tahrir
08:29:59 Feb 8

Sandmonkey Mahmoud Salem
People are heading out as early as 9 am. This will be massive. #jan25
08:43:49 Feb 8

tarekshalaby Tarek Shalaby
Mornin' revolution! Today at Tahrir, there's a 'garbage-collection party' and beautiful sunshine to keep us warm. #jan25
09:30:58 Feb 8

TravellerW Mo-ha-med
It's a beautiful day to take back our country. Good morning, #Egypt. #Jan25 #Tahrir
09:59:39 Feb 8

Striking Telecom workers
Photograph by @3arabawy Hossam el-Hamalawy - www.arabawy.org

3arabawy Hossam عمرو حسام
telecom workers in cairo r on strike. #egyworkers
11:25:21 Feb 8

3arabawy Hossam عمرو حسام
around 1000 workers in Lavarge Suez co r on strike. Among
their demands: forming union, supporting the revolution.
11:27:04 Feb 8

norashalaby Nora Shalaby
Looks like the workers are finally making a move. This is what
we need #Jan25
12:40:48 Feb 8

Professors march on Tahrir Square
Photograph by @3arabawy Hossam el-Hamalawy - www.arabawy.org

3arabawy Hossam عمرو حسام
3000 university professors r now marching on Tahrir from
Manyal. #jan25
12:52:4 Feb 8

3arabawy Hossam عمرو حسام
we r at least 10,000 now coming to u in Tahrir ya shabab!
Prepare the red carpets! :D #jan25
13:09:49 Feb 8

ashrafkhalil ashraf khalil
Today's chant by Tahrir welcoming committee: "Welcome o youth/freedom is at the gate" #Egypt
13:17:06 Feb 8

mosaaberizing Mosa'ab Elshamy
The owner of a travel agency in the square emptied his office and gave permission for doctors to use it as a clinic. #Jan25
13:25:13 Feb 8

3arabawy Hossam عمو حسام
haha i ca c the police like mice looking scared from the windows of their ministry building
13:41:30 Feb 8

3arabawy Hossam عمو حسام
a soldier now murmured to me: we r with u
14:06:50 Feb 8

3arabawy Hossam عمو حسام
can't stop myself from crying. We will win.
14:21:28 Feb 8

ashrafkhalil ashraf khalil
Another HUGE crowd in tahrir today. No sign yet of loss of momentum #egypt
14:59:35 Feb 8

monasosh monasosh
I am in a crowd shouting " to the parlimant" #Jan25
16:53:45 Feb 8

ashrafkhalil ashraf khalil
Tahrir protesters have officially outgrown the square and seeking to expand to new ground. defining moment. What will the army do? #egypt
16:56:48 Feb 8

monasosh monasosh
In a spontaneous march, heading to ppl's assembly, more r joining us on the way. Euphoria #Jan25
16:58:28 Feb 8

monasosh monasosh
Infront of ppl's assembly #Jan25 http://yfrog.com/h250larj

TravellerW Mo-ha-med
Yesterday it felt like #Tahrir was gearing up for war. Today it
really feels like we've won. #Egypt #jan25
17:04:45 Feb 8

ashrafkhalil ashraf khalil
#egypt when did tahrir security guys get laminated badges on
lanyards? Just noticed that. These guys are ORGANIZED!
17:12:48 Feb 8

monasosh monasosh
we are surrounding the ppl's assembly building. We'll take
back what is rightfully ours: Egypt #Jan25
17:36:08 Feb 8

monasosh monasosh
Right here was one of the most violent battles between us &
police on tue #Jan25 now it is totally ours
17:55:39 Feb 8

Cer Mohamed A. Hamama
This is the escalations we need right now.. YES! #tahrir
#jan25 #revolution
18:35:37 Feb 8

alaa Alaa Abd El Fattah
At last we are escalating #Jan25
18:37:06 Feb 8

RiverDryFilm Omar Robert Hamilton
The revolution rolls on! Stood among thousands who now control Parliament st - with several key ministries on it. #jan25 #egypt
18:51:53 Feb 8

Cer Mohamed A. Hamama
Chanting "By Friday noon, we will be inside the palace" in front of parliament #tahrir #Jan25 #Egypt
18:54:21 Feb 8

Cer Mohamed A. Hamama
Now I do feel it: #Mubarak will step down, no way out #tahrir #Jan25 #revolution #Egypt
18:56:14 Feb 8

Gsquare86 Gigi Ibrahim جيجي
Tahrir is one Egyptian melting pot ..I love it! The most numbers ever in liberation square all day and more are still coming in1
18:57:43 Feb 8

Gsquare86 Gigi Ibrahim جيجي
Actually Obama couldn't but YES WE (Egyptians) CAN! #Tahrir #Revolution http://yfrog.com/gyo2apdj

Cer Mohamed A. Hamama
I envy myself for witnessing this #revolution.. Ppl: u can't miss
what I am seeing here in #tahrir #Jan25 #Egypt
18:58:45 Feb 8

3arabawy Hossam عمرو حسام
We have no quarrel with the US people. We despise the US
govt, and its support for Israel and Arab dictators. We want
US troops out. #Jan25
18:59:19 Feb 8

ganzeer Ganzeer
Working on some Anti-Mubarak stencils and can't bring myself
to draw that nasty bastard's face. Eugh. #pukeinmouth #jan25
#tahrir #egypt
19:56:14 Feb 8

3arabawy Hossam عمرو حسام
Remember: The origin of the Egyptian pro-democracy
movement is the pro-Palestine and anti-War movements. The
local and the regional r linked
19:57:43 Feb 8

Ghonim Wael Ghonim
Dear Egyptians, Failure is not an option #Jan25
20:03:06 Feb 8

Milaakhir Adib
twitpic.com/3xr9rc Name: citizen Place of birth: Tahrir square D.O.B: 25
january 2011 Religion: egyptian Occupation: revolutionary

MohammedY Mohammed Yahia
What an eventful day! #Tahrir Square today is like no other day! It has never been this crowded since the very first day! #Jan25
20:12:28 Feb 8

beleidy Amr El Beleidy
So today Tahrir hit a new milestone, I know 8 people who went there for the first time, it seems a new wave of people are now taking part
20:22:53 Feb 8

monasosh monasosh
It's #Jan25 all over again. Ppl's excitement, their energy and determination overwhelming :)
21:27:31 Feb 8

tarekshalaby Tarek Shalaby
I want to rant about having a committee of older, experienced men represent the revolutionary youth & negotiate with the authorities #jan25
21:33:27 Feb 8

tarekshalaby Tarek Shalaby
1. These men are negotiating with the authorities, and none of us want this to happen until Mubarak is removed #jan25
21:36:03 Feb 8

tarekshalaby Tarek Shalaby
2. These men are not very aware of what the youth want, and there's a huge gap in terms of mentality, etc. #jan25
21:39:46 Feb 8

tarekshalaby Tarek Shalaby
3. Most of the youth they speak with are upper class, not too concerned with poverty, etc. And not the core protestors #jan25
21:41:3 Feb 8

tarekshalaby Tarek Shalaby
4. While their intentions are great, their methods are old-fashioned. We need to be progressive and revolutionary. We need change. #jan25
21:43:09 Feb 8

monasosh monasosh
I am happy I am happy I am happy ! #Jan25
21:45:58 Feb 8

MohammedY Mohammed Yahia
While today were the biggest protests, contrary to popular belief, I was not very happy with them. Kinda depressed to be honest #Jan25
22:15:19 Feb 8

MohammedY Mohammed Yahia
@theonevanished @zeitgeistbd @gryspnik My problem is sincerity. Ppl were there for the 'festive' atmosphere, not to overthrow Mubarak #Jan25
22:22:56 Feb 8

MohammedY Mohammed Yahia
I don't want our sincere msg to be diluted just for the sake of swelling numbers - at least that's how I feel (I may be wrong) #Jan25
22:28:16 Feb 8

monasosh monasosh
Setting up our own barricade and check points. Hehe so empowering #Jan25 http://yfrog.com/h05besmj
23:16:22 Feb 8

Cer Mohamed A. Hamama
Scenes from #Tahrir Square: The Welcome http://youtu.be/ K2866seHpWs #revolution #Egypt #Jan25
23:26:01 Feb 8

monasosh monasosh
Banner on parlimant's gate " closed till the regime is toppled" #Jan25 http://yfrog.com/h59l4zvyhcycfej
23:37:54 Feb 8

monasosh monasosh
An orange gets passed around whoever gets it has the turn to talk. Now talking abt resources of Egypt & limited jobs for youth #Jan25
00:21:40 Feb 9

Gsquare86 Gigi Ibrahim جيجي
I have zillion emails to reply to, endless photos/videos to upload & about hundreds of requests to confirm. Sleepy & exhausted..spare body?
00:33:44 Feb 9

pakinamamer Pakinam and Voice
I'll sleep better tonight knowing that #Tahrir's borders have expanded! Stay together, stay strong! Goodnight, Tweetville! x #Jan25 #Egypt
00:37:08 Feb 9

monasosh monasosh
And wt that my dear friends my mobilr battery dies. Good night from our new liberated area, the ppl's assembly is now wt the ppl :) #Jan25
04:16:19 Feb 9

17

WEDNESDAY, FEBRUARY 9
THE REVOLUTION DEEPENS

...as the organized working class joins the uprising

 Gsquare86 Gigi Ibrahim جيجي
Strike strike strike ..strike for the revolution!

THERE WAS AN UNINTENDED CONSEQUENCE *of the regime's back-to-normal policy — it gave workers returning to their jobs the opportunity to talk with their colleagues and act collectively. In countless factories and workplaces across Egypt they seized the chance to air long-held grievances. Their strikes combined economic demands with support for the Revolution.*

Strikes had begun previously, but by Wednesday they were everywhere. They paralyzed the government's whole strategy — to restart the economy, restore everyday life, and hope that people would forget about politics.

In fact Egypt had been experiencing a wave of strikes since 2006, brought on by neoliberal economic policies that suppressed wages and reduced job security. The abortive Mahalla strike of April 6, 2008, in which workers were killed by police, had inspired some of the activists involved in the January 25 uprising. Now it had come full circle — Tahrir Square had cracked the power of the regime, allowing labor to enter the arena.

Ghonim Wael Ghonim
This is not the time to "negotiate", this is the time to "accept" and "enforce" the demands of the Egyptian Youth movement #Jan25
06:41:38 Feb 9

Ghonim Wael Ghonim
An officer just called me to tell me: I escaped from the service after ElAdly asked us to fire live bullets randomly on protesters. #Jan25
07:29:17 Feb 9

alaa Alaa Abd El Fattah
1st lesson of the revolution, don't revolt in winter #Jan25
07:41:54 Feb 9

alaa Alaa Abd El Fattah
I say we take over parliament, not to increase pressure, but to have access to plugs so i can charge phone
08:07:44 Feb 9

mosaaberizing Mosa'ab Elshamy
Hundreds of protesters now sweeping the floors of Tahrir, others collecting garbage and some are washing the pavements.
09:21:06 Feb 9

Sandmonkey Mahmoud Salem
The police called saying they have found what's left of my car & need me to go to the station to get it. How about no? #jan25
09:23:24 Feb 9

Gsquare86 Gigi Ibrahim جيجي
Strike strike strike ..strike for the revolution!
11:02:43 Feb 9

Gsquare86 Gigi Ibrahim جيجي
To all students: DON'T GO BACK to ur universities and schools until the demands of the revolution are met
11:06:33 Feb 9

Gsquare86 Gigi Ibrahim جيجي
The strikes are everywhere ! Via @3arabawy
13:34:56 Feb 9

mosaaberizing Mosa'ab Elshamy
Army is in a good mood today, allowing all supplies through
Asr El Nil with minimum inspection and even making KFC
jokes. #Tahrir
14:21:29 Feb 9

alaa Alaa Abd El Fattah
In case u didn't get it organized labour joined the revolution,
wave of strikes sweeping country #Jan25
14:23:33 Feb 9

3arabawy Hossam عمو حسام
thousands of oil workers r now protesting in front of the oil
ministry. #jan25
15:04:40 Feb 9

3arabawy Hossam عمو حسام
at least 2 military production factories in Welwyn r on strike.
#jan25
15:06:27 Feb 9

3arabawy Hossam عمو حسام
several factories in suez have gone on strike. #jan25
15:07:56 Feb 9

3arabawy Hossam عمو حسام
the railway technicians in Bani Suweif r on strike. #jan25
15:11:44 Feb 9

3arabawy Hossam عمو حسام
shabab i can't keep up with the updates. There r strikes
everywhere! #jan25 #egyworkers
15:14:31 Feb 9

3arabawy Hossam عمو حسام
there is revolt taking place now in all state run newspapers by
journalists against their pro governest editors. #jan25
15:43:44 Feb 9

Sarahcarr أبو كار
Protest on the middle of downtown, blocked traffic, no police, workers forced uncooperative union official to leave. Just incredible.
16:22:50 Feb 9

TravellerW Mo-ha-med
#Egypt Gov already failing its promises. Only 1 of 3 'reform' committees formed, despite their pledge to formed two by yesterday. #Jan25
17:59:06 Feb 9

Cer Mohamed A. Hamama
Mother of the martyr Mohammad Mahmoud.. Looks devastated but insisting.. RIP #Jan25 #Tahrir http://twitpic.com/3xz96r

3arabawy Hossam عمو حسام
The police is cracking down brutally on the people in Kharga, Wadi el-Gedid Province. Live ammunition is being used on wide scale. #Jan25
18:16:57 Feb 9

Cer Mohamed A. Hamama
Protesters in #Tahrir are building a bathroom here in the square. #Egypt's revolution REALLY rocks #Jan25 #Revolution
19:21:51 Feb 9

pakinamamer Pakinam and Voice
Who would have thought that the Ministry of Interior would send us texts pleading with us and promising "honesty"? Mad times! #Jan25 #Egypt
20:37:04 Feb 9

TravellerW Mo-ha-med
#Jan25 #Egypt Ministry of Interior texting us: "From now on, we will only behave according to honesty, sincerity, & the rule of law".
20:54:06 Feb 9

tarekshalaby Tarek Shalaby
Over the past days, I've come to see Tahrir sq. as home, my little community. We recognise eachother now, and visitors stand out #jan25
21:33:34 Feb 9

tarekshalaby Tarek Shalaby
The workers' strikes throughout the republic is the missing element needed to succeed in the revolution. Vive la revolution! #jan25
00:19:12 Feb 10

18

THURSDAY, FEBRUARY 10
FURY

...when protesters' hopes are raised and dashed

 3arabawy Hossam عمرو حسام
People are waving their shoes in Tahrir Square, chanting:
LEAVE! LEAVE! #Jan25

TAHRIR WAS ALIVE WITH RUMORS. Was Hosni Mubarak about to resign? Soldiers with megaphones told the crowd that all their demands would be met. Then the Supreme Council of the Armed Forces appeared on TV – without its leader, the president.

No one knew what was going on. Had there been a military coup? Was that a good thing, or a backward step? Where was Mubarak? News agencies began reporting that he was to step down. The crowd became convinced. Detail aside, they had brought down the dictator. It was time to celebrate. Even President Obama said history was unfolding.

Then, running late, at a quarter-to-eleven at night, Mubarak's image appeared on the bedsheets used as a big screen in the Square. He did not look like a man who was about to resign as he repeated concessions that he had already made. Tahrir did not wait for the end of the speech. It exploded with rage.

Ghonim Wael Ghonim
I'm honored to represent 250k Egyptians to "convey" their demands to the Egyptian Government while collaborating with other activists #Jan25
07:59:08 Feb 10

alaa Alaa Abd El Fattah
I counted 16 different strikes in two days, 4 in factories owned by army, more to come #Jan25
08:03:43 Feb 10

alaa Alaa Abd El Fattah
Employees in 4 gvt departments held protests yesterday #Jan25
08:04:31 Feb 10

alaa Alaa Abd El Fattah
Hundreds of employees in state owned papers and tv revolting, leading to shift in discourse #Jan25
08:05:31 Feb 10

alaa Alaa Abd El Fattah
Proffessional syndicates and labour unions also on revolt kicking out regime figures from boards #Jan25
08:08:09 Feb 10

Cer Mohamed A. Hamama
Public transportation buses vanished from Cairo today as their workers went on strike. Revolution is rocking! #Jan25 #Egypt
08:40:56 Feb 10

Ghonim Wael Ghonim
I promise every Egyptian that I will go back to my normal life & not be involved in any politics once Egyptians fulfill their dreams. #Jan25
09:12:22 Feb 10

Cer Mohamed A. Hamama
#Workers are chanting: "Change.. Change.. The way is #Tahrir square" in front of ministry of oil #Jan25 #Egyworkers
09:14:48 Feb 10

Sandmonkey Mahmoud Salem
Tomorrow should be a nation-wide wake, a 20 million egyptian march in the memory of our fallen brothers & sisters. #jan25
09:31:37 Feb 10

mosaaberizing Mosa'ab Elshamy
It's day 17 of our revolution. Can't help but feel how near the end has become. Very optimistic about tomorrow. #Jan25
10:09:43 Feb 10

mosaaberizing Mosa'ab Elshamy
With the escalations growing, unprecedented numbers are expected to march tomorrow in what has been labelled 'Friday of Martyrs' #Jan25
10:27:00 Feb 10

Ghonim Wael Ghonim
It started to rain in Cairo, and I am optimistic. Hoping that sky is crying from happiness. #Jan25
12:49:43 Feb 10

ashrafkhalil ashraf khalil
Raining hard in Tahrir Square. Huge thunderclap and lighting--just made the protesters cheer even harder #egypt #jan25
13:45:25 Feb 10

alaa Alaa Abd El Fattah
Thunderstorm, again i'm humbled by fellow revolutionaries who do not leave the square even for a single night (i take regular breaks) #Jan25
13:50:32 Feb 10

alaa Alaa Abd El Fattah
Doctors marched in the morning from their syndicate wearing their white coats massive crowd joined #Jan25
14:41:56 Feb 10

Ssirgany Sarah El Sirgany
Govt responses r still on delay. We've moved to mass labor strikes while Suleiman is busy refuting 'democracy' statements. Too late!
14:49:50 Feb 10

norashalaby Nora Shalaby
Doctors marching in tahrir #Jan25 http://yfrog.com/h0mzkepj

Cer Mohamed A. Hamama
Number of people in #Tahrir square is huge despite this is not a 'million' day.. #Egypt #Jan25
15:59:10 Feb 10

Cer Mohamed A. Hamama
I just met my dad, mom and sister in #Tahrir.. My family is bringing #Mubarak down :D #Egypt #Jan25
16:22:20 Feb 10

Sandmonkey Mahmoud Salem
This might end tonite, hussam badrawy just said mubarak is coming on TV tonite to answer the people's demands. Fingers crossed. #jan25
16:33:57 Feb 10

Gsquare86 Gigi Ibrahim جيجي
My sister in #Tahrir square , that's huge
16:34:11 Feb 10

Cer Mohamed A. Hamama
High-rank army officer is now in #Tahrir talking to people.. I will try to know what is he saying #Egypt #Jan25
17:03:54 Feb 10

Cer Mohamed A. Hamama
Strangely, the army officer said that the protesters' demands
will be met by the night! #Egypt #Jan25 #Tahrir
17:20:09 Feb 10

Sandmonkey Mahmoud Salem
We dunno if this is good news yet. If u believe in god, its time
to pray. #jan25
17:24:02 Feb 10

Cer Mohamed A. Hamama
#Mubarak might step down by the night.. Ya Raaab!
17:24:58 Feb 10

Sandmonkey Mahmoud Salem
Speech from armed forces #jan25
17:25:38 Feb 10

Sandmonkey Mahmoud Salem
Statement # 1now #jan25
17:26:15 Feb 10

Sandmonkey Mahmoud Salem
They said nothing. Wtf? #jan25
17:27:03 Feb 10

3arabawy Hossam عمو حسام
We didn't fight and sacrifice all of this, so as to have the army,
which is ruling us from 1952, remains in power! #Jan25
17:30:00 Feb 10

ManarMohsen Manar Mohsen
Announcement from the military now: For the sake of
the interest + safety of Egypt, we will continue our role of
maintaining order. #Jan25
17:30:07 Feb 10

Ghonim Wael Ghonim
Mission accomplished. Thanks to all the brave young
Egyptians. #Jan25
17:31:00 Feb 10

3arabawy Hossam حسام عمو
WHAT ARE YOU TALKING ABOUT!??? RT: @Ghonim:
Mission accomplished. Thanks to all the brave young
Egyptians. #Jan25
17:35:11 Feb 10

Cer Mohamed A. Hamama
The blood of more than 300 martyrs can't be for the sake of
the army to take over.. #A7A
17:40:25 Feb 10

beleidy Amr El Beleidy
The PM said Mubarak might leave, now he is saying Mubarak
will stay, then he says nothing has been decided?!! What is
going on?!
17:43:47 Feb 10

Sandmonkey Mahmoud Salem
I am going to tahrir. It started there and will end there tonite.
#jan25
17:49:32 Feb 10

mosaaberizing Mosa'ab Elshamy
If it turns out the army will rule us now, we'll take a break for
the weekend and start another revolution. #Jan25
17:58:28 Feb 10

Packafy Pakinam Ahmed
The suspense is killing me! #Mubarak #Tahrir #jan25 #Military
#Martiallaw #Omarsuleiman #FREEDOM #FREEDOM
#FREEDOM
18:01:24 Feb 10

MennaAmr Menna Amr
This level of anticipation is worthy of the Jaws theme song.
#jan25
18:02:59 Feb 10

NevineZaki Nevine
Everybody, BREATHE
18:05:52 Feb 10

monasosh monasosh
Shit! What if he really steps down & takes wt him his bloody gang? We'll be back to normal life? But revolution is much more fun #Jan25
18:07:53 Feb 10

monasosh monasosh
Common ppl, be nice,atleast give us a chance to feel happy abt the possibility of him stepping down even if the battle isn't over yet #Jan25
18:26:29 Feb 10

Cer Mohamed A. Hamama
Millions of Egyptians are in #Tahrir right now CELEBRATING! #Egypt #Jan25
19:12:0 Feb 10

tarekshalaby Tarek Shalaby
Lucky and proud to be in Tahrir for this. Viva la revolucion! #jan25
19:24:18 Feb 10

Sandmonkey Mahmoud Salem
There isn't an empty inch in tahrir. #jan25
20:18:22 Feb 10

Sandmonkey Mahmoud Salem
Obama is on now #jan25
20:36:25 Feb 10

waelkhairy88 Wael Khairy
The regime & the army know they can't handle the 20 million estimated to march tomorrow which is why Mubarak will hopefully step down #EGYPT
20:57:59 Feb 10

waelkhairy88 Wael Khairy
Mubarak will address the nation at 10 o'clock, exactly an hour from now. Pray for a positive outcome. #Egypt
21:07:45 Feb 10

ashrafkhalil ashraf khalil
#egypt: wife tweeting for me as I am in Tahrir Square: mood is beyond Euphoric. Saw a Conga line chanting "Hosni's leaving Tonight" # jan25
21:23:37 Feb 10

ashrafkhalil ashraf khalil
#Jan25: If Mubarak somehow doesn't leave in an hour, Tahrir is going to explode. #egypt
21:24:56 Feb 10

ashrafkhalil ashraf khalil
#jan25: Chants from Tahrir Square "We're the internet youth; we're the youth of freedom". #egypt
21:31:58 Feb 10

Gsquare86 Gigi Ibrahim جيجي
Tahrir square is on fire, every inch of cement is covered with people chanting "Leave" "Invalid" Mubarak
21:41:27 Feb 10

ashrafkhalil ashraf khalil
#jan25: Tahrir square happiest place on earth. #egypt; so many Egyptians had given up on themselves and their ability to change things.
21:41:42 Feb 10

ashrafkhalil ashraf khalil
#egypt; Watching the Egyptians regain that sense of power and ownership is thrilling. I am starting to tear up; #jan25
21:42:45 Feb 10

Gsquare86 Gigi Ibrahim جيجي
Mubarak is a huge part of the regime, but not the only part, the regime must fall altogether !
21:44:41 Feb 10

Gsquare86 Gigi Ibrahim جيجي
Aljazeera: Ben Ali left after the 3rd speech, Mubarak only made 2 so far and tonight is the 3rd ..hmm :))
21:45:43 Feb 10

Sandmonkey Mahmoud Salem
15 min till mubarak speech. #finally #anticipation #neek.
#jan25
21:46:45 Feb 10

Gsquare86 Gigi Ibrahim جيجي
i can't describe my feelings, but i have waited for this for soo
long and i dreamed about it and it is happening ..Power of the
people :)
21:47:25 Feb 10

ashrafkhalil ashraf khalil
#egypt: more chants from Tahrir Square "The pilot, the pilot,
your plane awaits you" (all chants rhyme in Arabic so sound
better...): #jan25
21:52:33 Feb 10

3arabawy Hossam عمو حسام
The word "revolutionary" is not exclusive anymore to
"activists." Every Egyptian citizen is a revolutionary today.
#Jan25
22:00:56 Feb 10

pakinamamer Pakinam and Voice
Thank you universe for letting me be here, now, among the
revolutionaries. I couldn't wish for more. #Tahrir is glorious.
#Jan25
22:05:08 Feb 10

Sandmonkey Mahmoud Salem
Its not on. Goddamn it. They are late. #mubarakspeech
#jan25
22:05:14 Feb 10

HosniMobarak Hosni Mobarak
#reasonsmubarakislate: I'm aiming for an Oscar for the best
suspense movie. #Jan25 #Egypt
22:05:22 Feb 10

3arabawy Hossam عمو حسام
If he didnt step down tonight those 3 millions in Tahrir will
probably set themselves on fire. Now I know Mubarak's plan
to get rid of us!
22:17:14 Feb 10

3arabawy Hossam عمو حسام
FINALLY! Hosni is now on TV
22:46:15 Feb 10

3arabawy Hossam عمو حسام
A7a, he is not stepping down. We have to bring this fucker
from his palace and hang him in Tahrir Square. #Jan25
22:50:22 Feb 10

Sandmonkey Mahmoud Salem
He doesn't look like he is resigning. #jan25
22:50:57 Feb 10

ashrafkhalil ashraf khalil
#egypt speech on. Crowd realizing they're not going to hear
the magic words. This won't go well
22:53:42 Feb 10

ashrafkhalil ashraf khalil
#egypt; Still in Tahrir: Maybe I am projecting but the soldiers
watching speech don't look any happier than the crowd...
22:54:17 Feb 10

Sandmonkey Mahmoud Salem
" This has nothing to do with Hosny Mubarak " Hosny
Mubarak #jan25
22:58:42 Feb 10

mosaaberizing Mosa'ab Elshamy
Chanting against Mubarak now. Very angry chants. #Tahrir
22:59:43 Feb 10

3arabawy Hossam عمو حسام
People are waving their shoes in Tahrir Square, chanting:
LEAVE! LEAVE! #Jan25
22:59:45 Feb 10

3arabawy Hossam عمو حسام
Mubarak is playing a cheap game now, he's trying to imply if
he leaves it'll be coz of the Americans. It's too late to play this
card #Jan25
23:01:22 Feb 10

ashrafkhalil ashraf khalil
#egypt: more from Tahrir "He won't go until he's removed. So we'll remove him"
23:01:43 Feb 10

monasosh monasosh
As mubarak says this hideous speech, ppl in tahrir square r powerfully chanting " down wt Mubarak" #Jan25
23:02:18 Feb 10

Sandmonkey Mahmoud Salem
Mubarak is staying. The bastard is staying. #jan25
23:03:38 Feb 10

Sandmonkey Mahmoud Salem
People are going crazy in the street. We are joining them. #jan25
23:06:01 Feb 10

mosaaberizing Mosa'ab Elshamy
Hostile reactions in Tahrir now. Some waving shoes, others spitting on screens and women have broken into tears.
23:08:26 Feb 10

norashalaby Nora Shalaby
Fuck you Mubarak. No one believes ur lies here in #tahrir #Jan25 down w Mubarak
23:09:05 Feb 10

ashrafkhalil ashraf khalil
#egypt: New Chant from Tahrir "The people demand the trial of the president" #jan25
23:11:36 Feb 10

ManarMohsen Manar Mohsen
On my way to Tahrir Square. Never felt as angry as I do now.
23:12:28 Feb 10

waelkhairy88 Wael Khairy
Tomorrow #Egypt will take a plunge into chaos, and I don't mean similarly to last Friday, I mean complete anarchy! Stay safe loved ones.
23:18:37 Feb 10

waelkhairy88 Wael Khairy
The army is at a critical point. They'll either go against the people to defend the presidential palace tomorrow or march with us. #EGYPT
23:23:53 Feb 10

mosaaberizing Mosa'ab Elshamy
This pathetic speech migh've just pushed people to the edge now. Thousands calling for a march to presidential palace tomorrow. #Jan25
23:38:25 Feb 10

HosniMobarak Hosni Mobarak
Ha! Gotcha, again! Come on, you can't be that stupid. #Jan25 #Egypt
23:39:48 Feb 10

ashrafkhalil ashraf khalil
#egypt: Another chant, "Bukra Al Asr, Nirooh 3al Qasr".. Tomorrow afternoon, we march to the Palace (also rhymes of course)
23:46:04 Feb 10

monasosh monasosh
We r heading to the TV building "Maspiro" join us now and circulate #Jan25
23:54:16 Feb 10

alaa Alaa Abd El Fattah
Anger swelling after mubarak's arrogance 5000 protesters surround state tv building also close to tahrir #Jan25
00:08:30 Feb 11

alaa Alaa Abd El Fattah
We never start violence, the idea is to disable state tv but our numbers not big enough yet and building heavily baricaded #Jan25
00:16:44 Feb 11

monasosh monasosh
Stop telling us to keep it peaceful, we have always been peaceful & we r remaining peaceful. Any violence will be from Mubarak's ppl #Jan25
00:34:58 Feb 11

MohammedY Mohammed Yahia
We need to unite and be strong. Don't let #Mubarak get to you. At the end we are stronger and we will prevail while he falls #Jan25 #Tahrir
00:37:42 Feb 11

mosaaberizing Mosa'ab Elshamy
Protesters weren't even this shocked on Tue. & Wed. when martyrs fell. This is how sad Mubarak's speech has been. #Jan25
00:47:15 Feb 11

MohammedY Mohammed Yahia
I have seen #Mubarak singlehandedly let down 1 million ppl right in front of my eyes. I will not forgive for that #Jan25
01:01:26 Feb 11

Gsquare86 Gigi Ibrahim جيجي
Mubarak doesn't OWN Egypt !! Does he not understand the concept of a State?!
01:42:59 Feb 11

alaa Alaa Abd El Fattah
so now we have a sit in in front of tv building and a small one in front of president's residency in oroba hopefully tomorrow more #Jan25
02:39:00 Feb 11

monasosh monasosh
Ppl are chanting " here are the liars" while pointing at ppl looking at us from the TV building #Jan25
02:40:56 Feb 11

monasosh monasosh
Amazing energy, ppl just seem to recycle their anger into positive blasts of energy. Chants and drums & whistles all over #Jan25
02:43:00 Feb 11

alaa Alaa Abd El Fattah
people relax about this worry of crackdown, we are millions, they don't have anything that can effectively crackdown on us #Jan25
02:47:58 Feb 11

alaa Alaa Abd El Fattah
that doesn't mean they won't attempt something stupid, it
means it doesn't matter, let them attack we are ready #Jan25
02:48:36 Feb 11

ashrafkhalil ashraf khalil
one amazing aspect of tonight's debacle: it really seems like
Obama admin truly believed Mubarak would say something
different. #egypt
03:08:53 Feb 11

alaa Alaa Abd El Fattah
don't know what will happen. pre #Jan25 I could predict
tomorrow will be like today and yesterday, we revolt to gain
the right to unkown
04:26:48 Feb 11

alaa Alaa Abd El Fattah
I only know what WE WANT and what I WILL DO #Jan25
04:27:27 Feb 11

19

THE FRIDAY OF THE MARTYRS

...on which Mubarak falls

mosaaberizing Mosa'ab Elshamy
IT HAPPENED?!

THE ANGER OF THE PREVIOUS NIGHT had turned into apprehension. *Protesters had moved to surround the state TV building and were gathering outside the Presidential Palace. They feared that the army had sided with Mubarak — it was difficult to read the president's speech any other way. A bloodbath seemed a distinct possibility.*

Around midday the Supreme Council of the Armed Forces issued its second communiqué. Its meaning was unclear.

Behind the scenes something had gone wrong. Mubarak's speech had not been what the White House was expecting. Perhaps he had surprised the army too.

What was now beyond any doubt was that the People were one in demanding the fall of the regime. After Friday prayers the numbers protesting swelled. All Egypt was on the streets, their force was irresistible. Mubarak's authority existed in name only.

At 6:00 pm Vice President Suleiman appeared on state TV. He spoke for just a few seconds. Mubarak had resigned the office of president.

For the second time in twenty-four hours Tahrir exploded, this time with joy.

That night the whole of Egypt was Tahrir Square.

ashrafkhalil ashraf khalil
5:15 am, and I can still hear the drumming and chants from Tahrir from my balcony."Not afraid, Not afraid!" You gotta love these guys #egypt
05:20:56 Feb 11

mosaaberizing Mosa'ab Elshamy
Today is the third Friday of our revolution. The first was bloody, second was festive and third should be decisive. #Jan25
08:23:19 Feb 11

Salamander Sally Sami
In #tahrir with the pple of #egypt. If they were to kill us today I would die next to my brothers and sisters. I have no regrets. #jan25
10:55:01 Feb 11

Sandmonkey Mahmoud Salem
Please don;t think people will stop if the army joins sides w/ the president. We are just hoping the situation resolves without blood #jan25
11:45:36 Feb 11

MohammedY Mohammed Yahia
2nd army statement: Emergency law will be abolished "after current events are over"
11:49:00 Feb 11

MohammedY Mohammed Yahia
2nd army statement: The army promises fair elections and to oversee the modifications to the constitution.
11:50:02 Feb 11

MohammedY Mohammed Yahia
What a letdown. I can't believe I have been waiting for this army statement since last night hoping the army will side with ppl #Jan25
11:52:06 Feb 11

3arabawy Hossam عمو حسام
The second statement by the Armed Forces Council is BS. All promises in the future. I'm heading to Tahrir #Jan25
11:53:07 Feb 11

Sandmonkey Mahmoud Salem
The regular people might start seeing people protesting to
be unnecessary anymore, since the army guaranteed their
demands. #jan25
12:04:23 Feb 11

Sandmonkey Mahmoud Salem
This will be our greatest division yet. I hope the people will
remain united no matter what. #jan25
12:05:08 Feb 11

alaa Alaa Abd El Fattah
at least numbers in tahrir not going down, I don't expect the
gvt silly attempts will have any effect we will overcome
12:36:40 Feb 11

Sandmonkey Mahmoud Salem
The emergency law isn't lifted. It will be lifted once "calm
is restored" , which could mean after all of us are arrested.
#jan25
12:38:20 Feb 11

Gsquare86 Gigi Ibrahim جيجي
I am literally stuck in Tahrir, sooo many people, I will see the
possibility of starting a march to presidential palace
12:41:17 Feb 11

Ghonim Wael Ghonim
All my comments on TV stations asking people to celebrate
and go home was when everyone thought that its over
#Jan25
13:15:55 Feb 11

waelkhairy88 Wael Khairy
THe most crowded Friday prayer just ended. Some are
headed to Tahrir and others to the presidential palace. Lines
and lines of people #Egypt
13:29:16 Feb 11

waelkhairy88 Wael Khairy
Friday after Friday I keep saying it's the biggest protest yet,
but today it's truly epic. This is as massive as they come.
#EGYPT
13:56:37 Feb 11

mosaaberizing Mosa'ab Elshamy
Just joined thousands now marching from Tahrir to State TV
to join others there. #Jan25
14:06:45 Feb 11

monasosh monasosh
#Jan25 Reminder all Egypt protesting RT @Zeinobia:
Protests in Cairo , Alexandria,Mansoura,Damnhur, Tanta,
Mahalla, Asuit, Sohag, Bani sawfi
14:09:44 Feb 11

monasosh monasosh
Do not believe rumors of tension. Yes TV building is filled wt
heavily armed army men but they are as useless as ever till
now #Jan25
14:13:03 Feb 11

beleidy Amr El Beleidy
Can the people with rumours please chill? Yesterday we had
enough rumours for another 30 years!
14:16:09 Feb 11

SultanAlQassemi Sultan Al Qassemi
You know you're in trouble when: Iraq embassy in Cairo urges
Iraqis to return home http://bit.ly/gf4LOP
14:27:35 Feb 11

Cer Mohamed A. Hamama
Walking in #Tahrir, looking at faces of martyrs in their poster. A
human life, a human dream has ended thanks to Mubarak
14:33:07 Feb 11

3arabawy Hossam عمو حسام
tanks in front of the tv building. 1st floor soldiers have
stationed machine guns pointed in our direction. #jan25
14:40:04 Feb 11

Ghonim Wael Ghonim
Dear President Mubarak your dignity is no longer important,
the blood of Egyptians is. Please leave the country NOW.
#Jan25
14:43:13 Feb 11

mosaaberizing Mosa'ab Elshamy
The barricades at State TV were totally blocked but starting
to open up under pressure. Thousands joining. #Jan25
#Maspero
14:48:00 Feb 11

mosaaberizing Mosa'ab Elshamy
Note: Maspero is the common name given for State Tv
building. Will use it as it's shorter.
14:52:45 Feb 11

mosaaberizing Mosa'ab Elshamy
About 50,000 protesters now gathered just in few hours.
#Jan25 #Maspero
14:56:24 Feb 11

State TV building
Photograph by @3arabawy Hossam el-Hamalawy - www.arabawy.org

TravellerW Mo-ha-med
After a morning of worried indecision, the levels of energy at
#Tahrir are back to 11. On a 1 to 10 scale! #Egypt #jan25
15:19:03 Feb 11

mosaaberizing Mosa'ab Elshamy
Protesters at Maspero have already established inspection
lines and a medical point, showing they're in control of the
area now. #Jan25
15:20:03 Feb 11

Sandmonkey Mahmoud Salem
Heard from my aunt who lives next to the palace that the protesters are "very chic". Freakin heliopolis. :p #jan25
15:32:01 Feb 11

Gsquare86 Gigi Ibrahim جيجي
Mubarak is officially on a plane which doesn't change the situation ..Omar Suileman, Mubarak, & this regime are all illegitimate
15:42:29 Feb 11

Sandmonkey Mahmoud Salem
Very upscale crowd. Even the well off want mubarak gone. #jan25
15:43:10 Feb 11

Sandmonkey Mahmoud Salem
Need more protesters on the salah salem side. There are only 1000 there with thousands on the roxy side. Pl retweet #jan25
15:52:30 Feb 11

beleidy Amr El Beleidy
Egyptian State TV is still at it, all the demands have been met, people should go home! #Jan25
16:37:17 Feb 11

beleidy Amr El Beleidy
So we're waiting now for a statement from the presidency (Omar Suleiman), so far no statements have been fruitful
16:41:05 Feb 11

Gsquare86 Gigi Ibrahim جيجي
When Helioples rises-up demanding Mubarak to leave, you know that the end of Mubarak is very near :)
17:08:26 Feb 11

Sandmonkey Mahmoud Salem
I can also see mubarak residence airport. 5 helicopters used to be there, only 1 left on the ground & it's running. #jan25
17:11:35 Feb 11

beleidy Amr El Beleidy
So we are waiting for statements from both the army and the presidency, are we seeing a race to preempt one another?
17:15:56 Feb 11

Zeinobia Zeinobia
Al Arabiya : nearly 20 million Egyptians are in the street today
#Jan25
17:35:31 Feb 11

monasosh monasosh
I love how taking photos by the army tanks became a must for
all egyptian families #Jan25
17:45:27 Feb 11

beleidy Amr El Beleidy
Embarrassing parts of revolution: There was a battle with
camels & horses, and soon takes hours, thank you regime for
helping the stereotype
17:53:29 Feb 11

mosaaberizing Mosa'ab Elshamy
Wait, there's another 'urgent' speech in a while? Please, God,
no. #Jan25
17:53:52 Feb 11

beleidy Amr El Beleidy
Omar Sueliman speaking now!
18:02:18 Feb 11

3arabawy Hossam عمو حسام
Mubarak has stepped down, says Omar Suleiman. #Jan25
18:02:49 Feb 11

MennaAmr Menna Amr
WHAT THE FUCK!
18:02:51 Feb 11

beleidy Amr El Beleidy
I cannot believe what just happened! Hosny Mubarak
resigned! The army now controls the country!
18:03:42 Feb 11

mosaaberizing Mosa'ab Elshamy
IT HAPPENED?!
18:04:19 Feb 11

3arabawy Hossam عمرو حسام
Gunshots in Nasr City. Everyone is celebrating. #Jan25
18:04:51 Feb 11

MennaAmr Menna Amr
WE DID IT! #jan25 #surreal
18:04:55 Feb 11

Sandmonkey Mahmoud Salem
Honsy quit . We won. We won :) #jan25
18:05:19 Feb 11

Cer Mohamed A. Hamama
Mubarak to step down.. I am not able to breathe #Jan25
#Egypt
18:06:10 Feb 11

Packafy Pakinam Ahmed
YAAAAAAAAAAAAAAAAAAAAAAAAAAAAAAAAAAAAAAAAAAAAY
#jan25 #FREEDOM
18:07:43 Feb 11

ManarMohsen Manar Mohsen
Goodbye, Mubarak!
18:08:02 Feb 11

mosaaberizing Mosa'ab Elshamy
Tears filling Tahrir!
18:08:14 Feb 11

3arabawy Hossam عمرو حسام
We got rid of Mubarak. Now it's time to get rid of the
Mubarak's regime. Long live the Egyptian people. Long live
the revolution. #Jan25
18:09:54 Feb 11

ManarMohsen Manar Mohsen
Who did this? WE did, the people. Without guns. Without
violence. Rather, with principles and persistence. Mabrouk,
everyone!
18:11:01 Feb 11

mosaaberizing Mosa'ab Elshamy
It IS the decisive Friday. I'm only crying at the moment along with 2 million men in Tahrir.
18:12:00 Feb 11

monasosh monasosh
Shit! Ppl are going crazy, screaming and running, Mubarak jas stepped down #Jan25
18:12:41 Feb 11

monasosh monasosh
Ppl are screaming " long live the revolution" we finally got rid of him #Jan25
18:14:37 Feb 11

Ghonim Wael Ghonim
The real hero is the young Egyptians in Tahrir square and the rest of Egypt #Jan25
18:14:57 Feb 11

TravellerW Mo-ha-med
Egypt, the Middle East, the World will never be the same. From #Tahrir square - CONGRATULATIONS, FREE #EGYPT! #jan25
18:15:14 Feb 11

monasosh monasosh
we got rid of Mubarak! Egypt won! #Jan25
18:17:28 Feb 11

Reem_Ahmed Reem Ahmed Shalaby
Oh God !! deep breathe !!! Freedom :)))) #Tahrir #Jan25 #Egypt , we have made it. thanks God :))
18:18:34 Feb 11

NevineZaki Nevine
Its crazy!! The streets are craaaaaaaaaaaaaaaazyyyyyyy!!!!
18:18:58 Feb 11

ashrafkhalil ashraf khalil
Amazing, just amazing! Part of me never truly believed, even yesterday, that this could happen #egypt #jan25
18:19:25 Feb 11

waelkhairy88 Wael Khairy
MABROOK FELLOW EGYPTIANS! We made it!!! Cheers and millions hopping up and down. Cars honking their horns. Smiles all over. I'm speechless.
18:20:22 Feb 11

ashrafkhalil ashraf khalil
And there's a bonus: Egyptians now get to brag that they got rid of their guy faster than the Tunisians. WE WIN!! #Egypt #jan25
18:25:29 Feb 11

HosniMobarak Hosni Mobarak
You're welcome. #Egypt #Jan25
18:29:07 Feb 11

3arabawy Hossam عمو حسام
I want to send a BIG THANK YOU to @AjEnglish and @ AjArabic. You bravely aired our revolution to the rest of the world. #Jan25
18:29:10 Feb 11

3arabawy Hossam عمو حسام
And I'd like to send a big FUCK YOU to the Egypt State TV. You'll be on trial soon. #Jan25
18:29:34 Feb 11

ashrafkhalil ashraf khalil
The new record stands at 18 days for hounding out an entrenched dictatorship. Who is the Middle East is next? #egypt #jan25
18:29:51 Feb 11

Sandmonkey Mahmoud Salem
Peopke jumping up and down. Everyone hugging. We did it. I wanna cry from happiness. #jan25
18:31:10 Feb 11

norashalaby Nora Shalaby
In 18 days we got rid of the ruthless dictator Mubarak!!! Go Egypt! #Jan25
18:37:00 Feb 11

MohammedY Mohammed Yahia
Lets not forget those who fell during the past 18 days. This victory, as sweet as it is, is dedicated to you. It is the most precious #Jan25
18:38:43 Feb 11

monasosh monasosh
Today we fulfilled our promise to those who died #Jan25 #KhaledSaid
18:44:23 Feb 11

MohammedY Mohammed Yahia
Liberated lands: Tunisia, Egypt. Next on the map: Algeria, Jordan, Yemen, Syria - and maybe even Saudi Arabia! WE DESERVE IT! #Jan25
18:50:16 Feb 11

monasosh monasosh
I can't stop crying & laughing #Jan25
18:50:24 Feb 11

MohammedY Mohammed Yahia
I have vowed when we started if I see this through,I'll do my best to rebuild this country into the beauty it deserves. I start today #Jan25
18:53:01 Feb 11

MennaAmr Menna Amr
The best part? He stepped down on the day dedicated to the martyrs. Their lives were not lost in vain. 11/2/2011 #jan25 #victory
18:56:47 Feb 11

Sandmonkey Mahmoud Salem
FIREWORKS, CELEBRATIONS, FUN! JUBILATION! I AM NOT MAKING SENSE. I AM HEADING TO TAHRIR! #JAN25
18:57:05 Feb 11

Sandmonkey Mahmoud Salem
To everyone who rediculed us, opposed us, wanted us to compromise, i say: YOU ARE WELCOME :) TODAY WE ALL CELEBRATE!!! #JAN25
18:58:33 Feb 11

beleidy Amr El Beleidy
Walking to tahrir now!
18:58:41 Feb 11

Sandmonkey Mahmoud Salem
I WANT KFCCCCCC!!!! #JAN25
19:10:29 Feb 11

Cer Mohamed A. Hamama
I want someone to hold me.. We made Mubarak to step
down.. Long live our revolution :D #Egypt #Jan25 #Tahrir
19:11:37 Feb 11

ManarMohsen Manar Mohsen
The streets in Cairo are going wild with patriotism &
happiness! Flags waving out of every car, strangers
congratulating each other! "MASR!"
19:29:12 Feb 11

norashalaby Nora Shalaby
Fireworks!! #Jan25
19:30:21 Feb 11

Ghonim Wael Ghonim
No more torture in Egypt. #Jan25
19:44:48 Feb 11

Sandmonkey Mahmoud Salem
Now let's remove his fuckin name from everything. I don't
wanna hear the word mubarak ever again #jan25
19:52:38 Feb 11

Ghonim Wael Ghonim
They lied at us. Told us Egypt died 30 years ago, but millions
of Egyptians decided to search and they found their country in
18 days #Jan25
19:53:33 Feb 11

Sandmonkey Mahmoud Salem
The police is nowhere to be seen. Let's hope they left as well.
#jan25
20:04:12 Feb 11

Gsquare86 Gigi Ibrahim جيجي
I can't stop crying. I've never been more proud in my life
20:10:39 Feb 11

Gsquare86 Gigi Ibrahim جيجي
i was suppose to graduate today from AUC, i am proud to say
that i am having the best party ever!!! Feb 11, 2011
20:13:43 Feb 11

3arabawy Hossam حسام و عمو
I can't recall how many times we thought we 're about to b
massacred & our revolution 'd be squashed. Still the will of
the people prevailed
20:14:39 Feb 11

Gsquare86 Gigi Ibrahim جيجي
Tahrir square is on fire out of happiness, pride, and
celebration ..i wish you were all with me !
20:16:37 Feb 11

Celebrating in Tahrir Square
Photograph by @ramyraoof Ramy Raoof - www.ebfhr.blogspot.com

monasosh monasosh
Ppl are chanting " Egypt is free, mubarak out" & " we r the
youth of revolution" & " raise ur head, u r an Egyptian" #Jan25
20:17:07 Feb 11

Gsquare86 Gigi Ibrahim جيجي
We must continue to give and ensure that this victorious revolution translates into real democracy
20:21:23 Feb 11

Gsquare86 Gigi Ibrahim جيجي
Thank you Tunisians 4m the bottom of my heart. Algeria, Yemen, Jordan, Palestine, Saudi, Syria & Libya:keep fighting, nothing is impossible
20:24:59 Feb 11

mosaaberizing Mosa'ab Elshamy
Oh, and hundreds of those celebrating never joined the protests before. But it's alright, we're all Egyptians :)
20:26:24 Feb 11

Gsquare86 Gigi Ibrahim جيجي
Time to go celebrate before the real hard work begins..Viva Egypt
20:28:28 Feb 11

mosaaberizing Mosa'ab Elshamy
Army just made a 3rd announcement. Promising stuff. Most emotional part was when spokesman paid tribute to the martyrs. Mubarak never did.
20:30:21 Feb 11

Ghonim Wael Ghonim
The military statement is great. I trust our Egyptian Army #Jan25
20:31:02 Feb 11

Ghonim Wael Ghonim
Please don't make me the face of this revolution. Its not true as every Egyptian was the face of this revolution #Jan25
20:51:17 Feb 11

monasosh monasosh
Unbelievable the metro driver is cheering wt the horn, ppl are dancing & screaming in the metro station #Jan25
20:55:56 Feb 11

monasosh monasosh
We just scratched out "Mubarak" name from metro-stations map & replaced it wt " the martyrs" #Jan25 http://yfrog.com/gy4vuuj
21:11:21 Feb 11

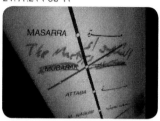

3arabawy Hossam عمرو حسام
To Palestinians who r thanking me, I need to thank u. My introduction to politics was the Palestinian cause. We'll never forget Palestine.
21:14:10 Feb 11

Sandmonkey Mahmoud Salem
My aunt-who lives next to Mubarak- told me the guards started firing in celebration the moment he left. REVOLUTION! #JAN25
21:20:14 Feb 11

beleidy Amr El Beleidy
If u ever thought tahrir was crowded u should see it now!
21:20:14 Feb 11

3arabawy Hossam عمرو حسام
In dictatorship, independent journalism by default becomes a form of activism, the spread of information is essentially an act of agitation.
21:32:29 Feb 11

beleidy Amr El Beleidy
After taking down Mubarak, I cannot think of anything that is not possible!
22:15:40 Feb 11

MohammedY Mohammed Yahia
I will go tom to clean up Tahrir. I'm willing to do anything!
Clean up, painting - anything for the most special place to my
heart #Jan25
23:23:54 Feb 11

mosaaberizing Mosa'ab Elshamy
I thought I would finally be able to get some sleep but the
partying only gets louder with time :) #Tahrir #Jan25
23:32:21 Feb 11

monasosh monasosh
We should go & celebrate infront of omraneya police station.
They were famous for torturing ppl #Jan25
23:42:32 Feb 11

monasosh monasosh
I'm in Tahrir square.This is where it all started on #Jan25
when we declared our demands ppl thought we were mad.
Look where madness got us
00:31:48 Feb 12

Sandmonkey Mahmoud Salem
Guys, tomorrow we free all of our detainees. And clean up
tahrir square :) #jan25
00:32:40 Feb 12

3arabawy Hossam عمرو حسام
People we will get free press. We fought for it, and we got it.
NO RED LINES ANYMORE! #Jan25 #Press #Journalists
01:38:57 Feb 12

MohammedY Mohammed Yahia
Ppl asked us 2 stop so Mubarak has a dignified exit.I'm glad
we didn't. Anything less wouldn't have been dignified for our
martyrs #Jan25
01:43:53 Feb 12

MohammedY Mohammed Yahia
And personally,I find the rights of our martyrs who died for
freedom r 1000 times more important than Mubarak. 2day
they're dignified #Jan25
01:46:52 Feb 12

suzeeinthecity su zee
My dad hugged me after the news and said 'Ur generation
did what ours could only dream of. i'm sorry we didn't try hard
enough.' #egypt
01:52:17 Feb 12

monasosh monasosh
Tomorrow 10am, we all go and help in cleaning tahrir square.
Bring garbage bags, gloves and join us #Jan25
02:11:25 Feb 12

Ghonim Wael Ghonim
Dear Egyptians, Go back to your work on Sunday, work like
never before and help Egypt become a developed country.
#Jan25
03:17:28 Feb 12

monasosh monasosh
Too tired to celebrate. Managed 2 see most of my beloved
friends & family to give them a hug. Sleep & tomorrow it'll all
soink in :)
03:51:03 Feb 12

Cer Mohamed A. Hamama
To live a revolution! #Egypt #Jan25
04:12:09 Feb 12

Gsquare86 Gigi Ibrahim جيجي
No more lies, no more contradictions, no more dictatorship, I
can't sleep realizing what we did #proudegyptian
04:35:00 Feb 12

TravellerW Mo-ha-med
It's 4:30 AM. I think it's an excellent time to call and annoy
all people who have been telling us to leave the square. :)
#Egypt #Jan25
04:38:14 Feb 12

Gsquare86 Gigi Ibrahim جيجي
I was honored today to finally meet and talk with Khaled
Said's mom and uncle who were the proudest people, we
cried, it was so moving
04:40:19 Feb 12

TravellerW Mo-ha-med
Favourite moment on the square tonight: "مش هانمشي، القعدة حلوة"
"we're not leaving, we like it here!" #Egypt #Jan25 #Victory
04:44:15 Feb 12

TravellerW Mo-ha-med
I'll be very honest: I am in complete disbelief about what
happened today. Hasn't sunk in yet. #Egypt #Jan25
04:45:05 Feb 12

Gsquare86 Gigi Ibrahim جيجي
There must be a #Jan25 revolution monument erected in
#Tahrir sq with the name of all the martyrs in the middle circle
#Egypt
04:48:07 Feb 12

Gsquare86 Gigi Ibrahim جيجي
The road to Jerusalem passes through Cairo, we are that
much closer. Palestine you will always be the greatest battle
of all
04:57:44 Feb 12

TravellerW Mo-ha-med
I hugged so many people I had never met until today!
#Victory! #Uniy #Egypt #Jan25
04:59:29 Feb 12

TravellerW Mo-ha-med
Now Ahmed, whose son Eslam was killed by the police &
who vowed not to leave #Tahrir until Mub. left, can go home.
#Egypt #Jan25 #Justice
05:08:31 Feb 12

20

THE CLEANUP

...as the Egyptian People begin anew

MohammedY Mohammed Yahia
Today I'm taking off my revolutionary role and shifting into cleaner role! Heading out to clean #Tahrir Square till it sparkles! #Jan25

ON THE MORNING AFTER Mubarak stepped down, activists returned to Tahrir Square to clean it. It was an expression of the sense of ownership of their country they now felt.

The army had taken power but its position was still unclear, despite promises that it would hand over power to a civilian government in due course. While the Supreme Council of the Armed Forces said all the Revolution's demands would be met, many detainees had still not been released, Egypt's emergency law remained in force and most of Mubarak's ministers continued on.

Activists debated whether the Tahrir occupation should be ended, and what form the next stage of the Revolution would take. These discussions would continue into the future, but for now the overwhelming feeling was one of pride.

Over the previous eighteen days, Egyptians had done something extraordinary. They had toppled the dictator.

Sandmonkey Mahmoud Salem
Good morning Egypt! Today you are free! :) #jan25
09:14:10 Feb 12

mosaaberizing Mosa'ab Elshamy
I haven't seen my bed in SO long, it's gonna be one hell of an emotional reunion :)
09:17:45 Feb 12

norashalaby Nora Shalaby
We want to form a tahrir committee - to clean it up, redesign it & set up a memorial for the martyrs #Jan25
10:38:06 Feb 12

MohammedY Mohammed Yahia
Today I'm taking off my revolutionary role and shifting into cleaner role! Heading out to clean #Tahrir Square till it sparkles! #Jan25
11:38:08 Feb 12

3arabawy Hossam عمو حسام
While middle class activists here on Twitter r urging Egyptians to return to work, the working class strikes and protests continue. #Jan25
11:49:43 Feb 12

Gsquare86 Gigi Ibrahim جيجي
Egypt clean-up, Mubarak out, and trash with him #Tahrir
http://yfrog.com/h7pmprxj

Sandmonkey Mahmoud Salem
This is nuts. Everyone is cleaning :)
12:29:15 Feb 12

TravellerW Mo-ha-med
#NewEgypt will be clean.
12:47:19 Feb 12

monasosh monasosh
Sun is shining on Tahrir square,everyone here is smiling and
cleaning. Beautiful people of my country #Jan25
12:47:32 Feb 12

norashalaby Nora Shalaby
On my way to tahrir from qasr el nil. Seems everyone's
cleaned everything up already! Great job guys #Jan25
12:56:52 Feb 12

sharifkouddous Sharif Kouddous
I bump into my cousin, Ismail Naguib, on Kasr El Nile bridge.
He says: "the new weapon of choice is the broom" #Tahrir
#Egypt
14:04:54 Feb 12

Sandmonkey Mahmoud Salem
The supreme military council has made its 4th announcement.
And it was good. #jan25
15:12:40 Feb 12

norashalaby Nora Shalaby
Have to say, not so happy w army's statement. Y r they
keeping the old gov. in place?
15:27:39 Feb 12

sharifkouddous Sharif Kouddous
People debating whether to leave #Tahrir following military
announcement that Mubarak cabinet staying place. #Egypt
15:59:01 Feb 12

Cer Mohamed A. Hamama
Egyptians are cleaning the army tanks in #Tahrir :)) #Egypt
#Jan25 #FreeEgypt
16:41:25 Feb 12

Gsquare86 Gigi Ibrahim جيجي
The revolution continues but outside Tahrir square , it will and
MUST continue but in different forms
19:38:51 Feb 12

Gsquare86 Gigi Ibrahim جيجي
Tahrir square gained us Mubarak to step down, now the real
resistance starts in factories, universities, towns, & streets
..level 2
19:40:17 Feb 12

Gsquare86 Gigi Ibrahim جيجي
Plus Tahrir is the people's square, we can always come and
sit-in if we find that our revolution is being hijacked
20:09:43 Feb 12

Sandmonkey Mahmoud Salem
Things I have learned those past few days: How to conduct
peaceful protests, how to survive riot police attacks, how to
deal with tear gas..
02:13:44 Feb 13

Sandmonkey Mahmoud Salem
What things to use to disable teargas effects, how to
catch teargas canisters, how rubber bullets really are like..
#thingsIvelearned
02:15:04 Feb 13

Sandmonkey Mahmoud Salem
How to organize a street gang, how to attack a guy with a
semi-automatic doing a drive-by, how to deal with a lynchmob,
#thingsIvelearned
02:16:45 Feb 13

Sandmonkey Mahmoud Salem
What the true nature of Egyptians really is like....and finally,
how to bring down a dictator. :D #ThingsIvelearned
02:18:22 Feb 13

mosaaberizing Mosa'ab Elshamy
Third night in a row where I dream of the young man who was sniped right before my eyes in #Tahrir. Shot straight in the head.
01:27:28 Feb 14

mosaaberizing Mosa'ab Elshamy
Another one was when thugs occupying a roof attacked us with molotov, a man climbed up and helped us get through. He never came back though.
01:49:36 Feb 14

mosaaberizing Mosa'ab Elshamy
Tahrir will always remain to be the place where I experienced the most depressing AND gleeful moments of my life.
01:56:39 Feb 14

21

EPILOGUE

EVEN BEFORE MUBARAK HAD GONE events in Egypt had inspired revolts elsewhere in the Arab world. The baton that had passed from Tunisia to Egypt was now flung out to be caught by any of the many peoples who were still living under dictatorship. First it was Yemen, then Algeria, Morocco, Bahrain, Libya, and elsewhere. It was impossible to predict where the next uprising would be.

Egyptians asked for and then distributed lists of tweeters for people to follow in the various countries, and retweeted their news with the hashtags for the different movements. A sense of international solidarity was forged online that was then taken to the streets in protests outside embassies in Cairo.

Unfortunately it seemed the lesson that most of these dictatorships took from Egypt was to act with even greater cruelty. There would be more deaths, more desperate acts of courage in the face of brutality, more setbacks, and yet, at the time of writing, no end to the fight against oppression.

Sandmonkey Mahmoud Salem
Dear Iran, algeria and Bahrain revolution tweeps, please let me know who u r, so I can follow u and retweet u.
16:33:22 Feb 16

monasosh monasosh
I feel like crying RT @hadeelalsh: Protesters in Pearl square singing #egypt national anthem #jan25 #bahrain #feb14
19:37:33 Feb 16

ShababLibya LibyanYouthMovement
our Egyptian brothers and sisters please help the Libyans, you have more numbers on the net, spread #Libya #Feb17 we need your help #egypt
01:21:52 Feb 17

monasosh monasosh
I need a good list to follow for #Bahrain & #libya any recommendations?
19:13:57 Feb 17

mxbw M
@monasosh for bahrain: twitter.com/#!/list/ThomasMeadia/... he has one for libya too
19:15:23 Feb 17

BahrainRights Bahrain Human Rights
Ambulances are being blocked from approaching pearl in #Bahrain by security forces...army open live fire...
17:42:53 Feb 18

ShababLibya LibyanYouthMovement
we did it we did it, benghazi is free, a sat channel will be on air shortly god willing, we did it OURSELVES thanks for all support
19:50:29 Feb 18

LibyanThinker The Libyan Thinker
@acarvin I have Egyptian Contact ready to cross into #Libya with food and med supplies. they need a libyan contact in the east to meet them.
00:04:13 Feb 20

libya2p0 بنغازي ليبيا
Urgent Libyans are in dangers, there is a massacre in
Benghazi no medical supply, the regime is trying to blackout
the media PLZ RT #FEB17
02:51:12 Feb 20

Not the End

HosniMobarak Hosni Mobarak
You people are hypocrites! You talk about democracy, but
you won't let me run for president? Where's the freedom?!
#VoteHosni #Egypt
18:52:09 Feb 13